Contemporary Israeli Artists

21 Tones of Color

Curator and album producer:
Bella Zaichik Shomer

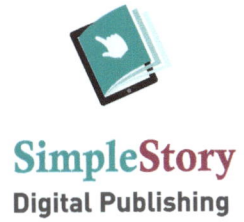

SimpleStory
Digital Publishing

Graphic Design: Smadar Munis

Translation: Grace Michaeli

Production: Simple story

www.simplestory.co.il

Copyright 2021 by BELLA ZAICHIK SHOMER

© All rights Reserved

All Image Rights are Reserved to Their Artists

First Edition

No part of this book may be reproduced, copied, photocopied, recorded, translated, stored in a database, transmitted or received, in any manner or by any electronic, optical, mechanical or other means. Commercial use of any kind of the material contained in this book is strictly prohibited, except with the express written permission of Bella Zaichik Shomer.

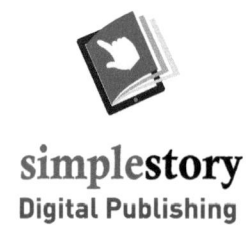

simplestory
Digital Publishing

This art album is dedicated with admiration and love to my grandchildren: Yalley and Danny, Yahav and Geffen, who are the color palette of my life.

October, 2021

Introduction

This art album, the first of an Israeli artists album series, presents works by 21 artists who live in Israel.

The process of globalization has gradually blurred the boundaries between the local and global. Israeli art vacillates between local issues and a dialogue with international steams of art. The art album presents Israeli scenery, portraits, sculptures, paintings and photographs, both abstract and realistic, all side by side.

Art that accepts the world as seen from the artists' inner personal world. Before us is a sensual depiction and cognitive burst or art through shapes and colors. Visual art that touches the heart and serves as a source of inspiration.

About the Curator and album producer

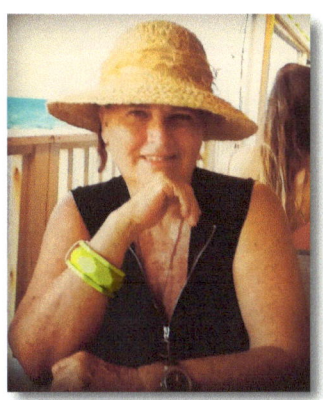

Bella Zaichik Shomer is a qualified curator of single and group exhibitions. Completed her MA in art history at the Hebrew University, focusing on art research and criticism. Former curator at The Israel Museum and Yad VaShem Museum. Has curated the permanent exhibitions at the Menachem Begin Heritage Center and at the Yad Mordechai Museum. Has curated dozens of single and group exhibitions at leading galleries in Israel and abroad.

The Artists

Dina Luzon Zaifer 8

Smadar Unna 10

Dalia Rotem 12

Yakov Korenblum 14

Dorit Amit 16

Michal Agmon Gonnen 18

Shay Aloni 20

Miriam Cojocaru 22

Yair David 24

Shlomo Emanuel 26

Ilan Goldstein 28

Michal Goren 30

Irit Haskin 32

Ricki Maissy 34

Tammara Or 36

Ishay Rossano 38

Liora Shaham 40

David Tsinman 42

Anna Tufeld 44

Netiva Caftori 46

Varda Breger 48

Dina Luzon Zaifer

- Drawing. Sculpture
- dina.zaifer@gmail.com
- www.dina-zaifer.wixsite.com/artist
- Facebook: dina zaifer

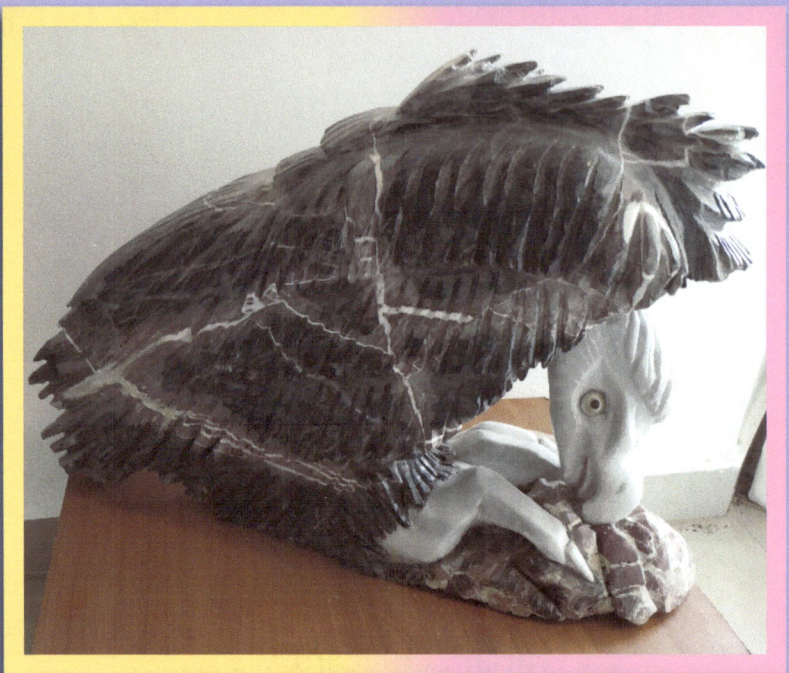

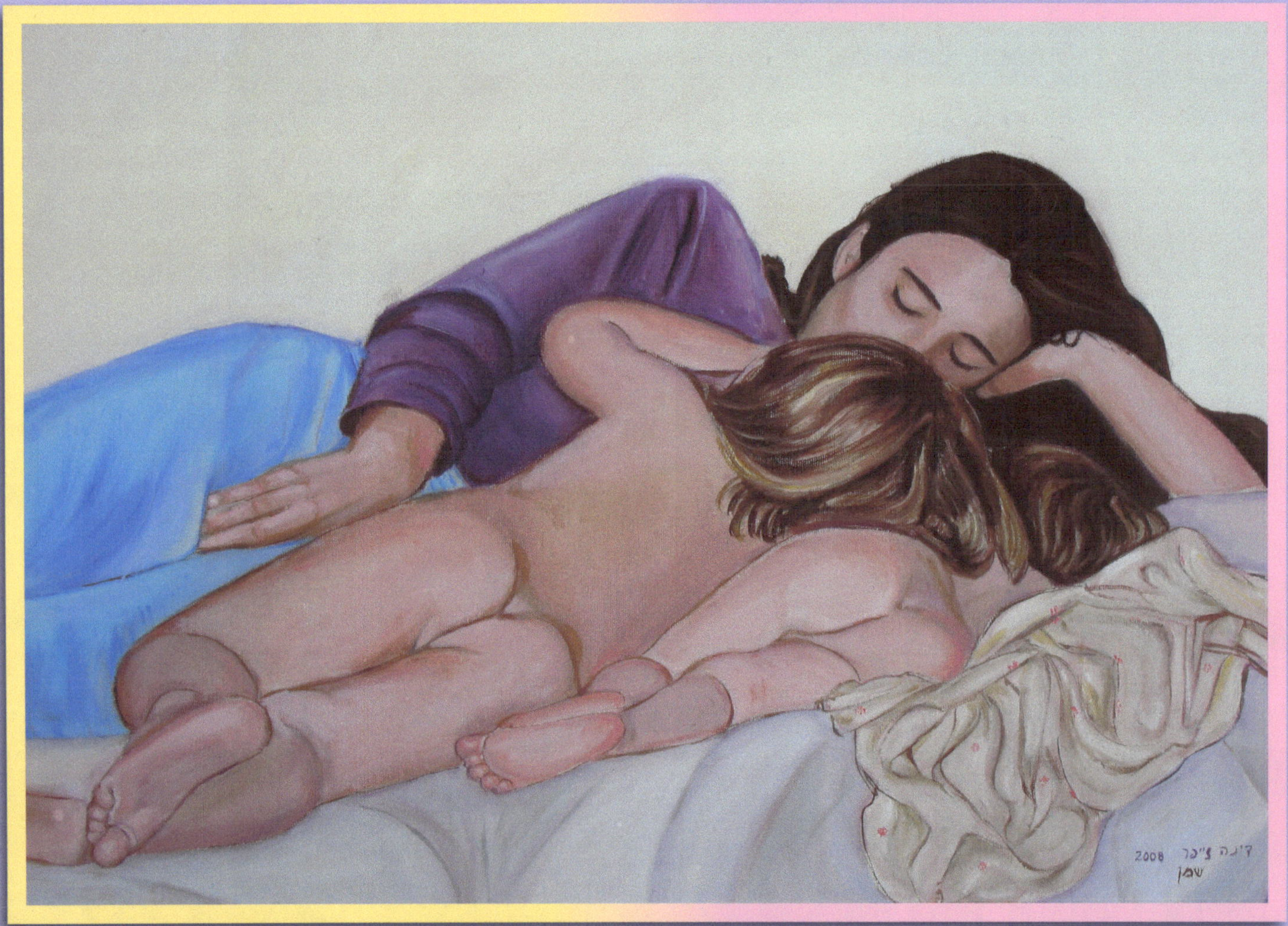

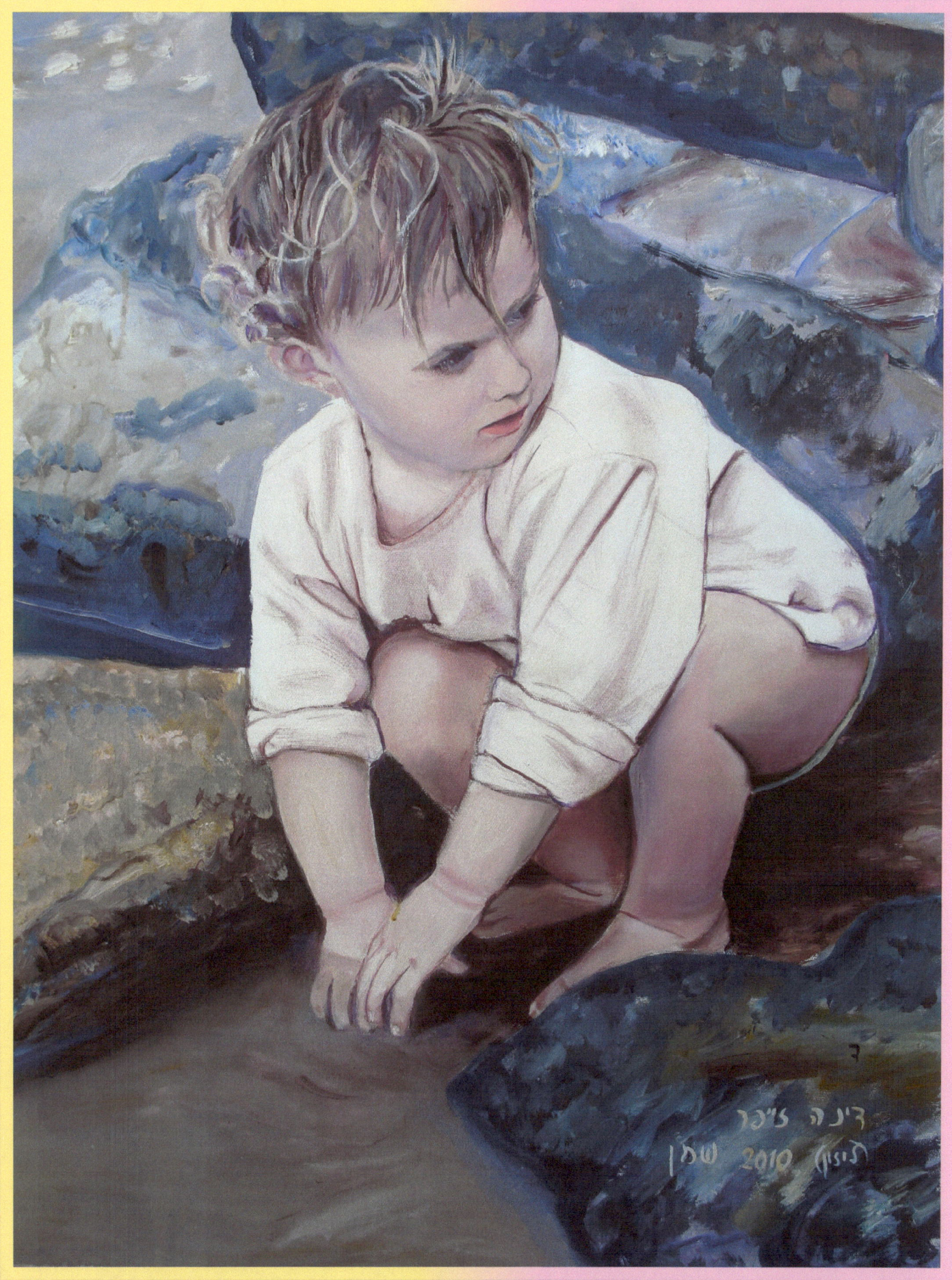

Smadar Unna

- Painting
- smadar.unna@gmail.com
- www.unnast.com

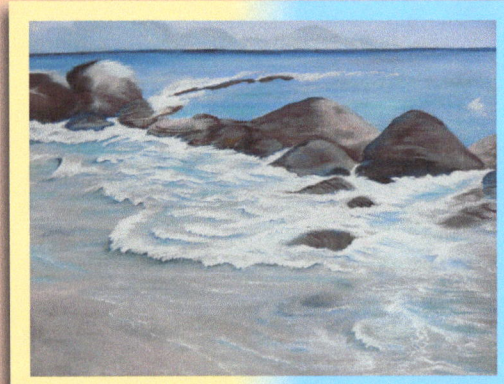
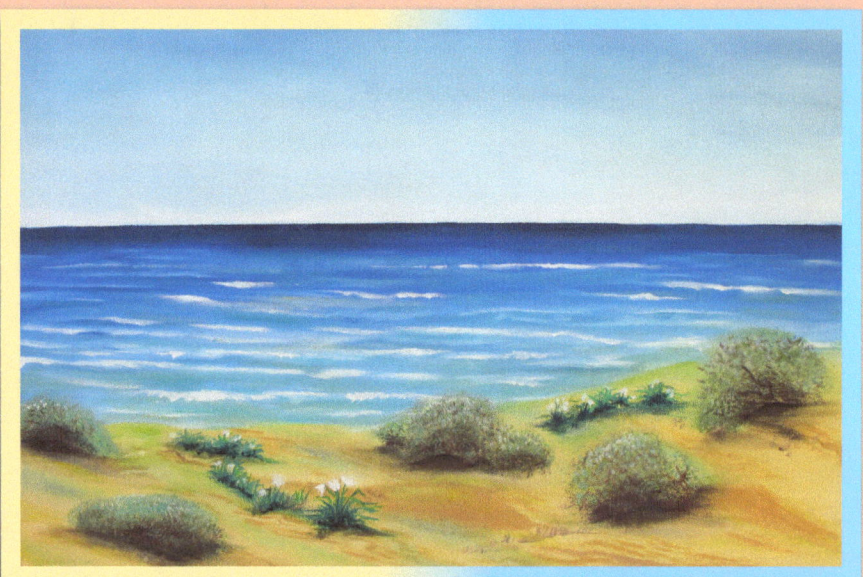
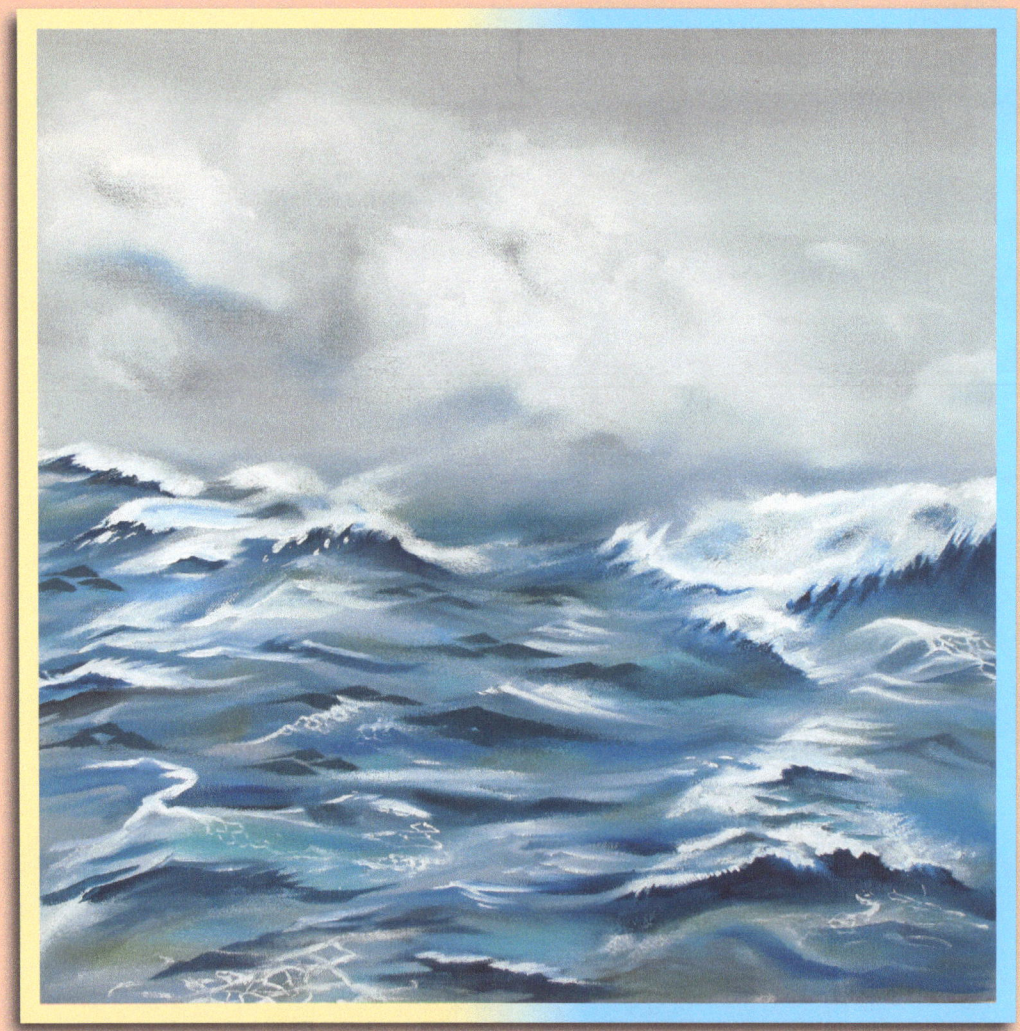

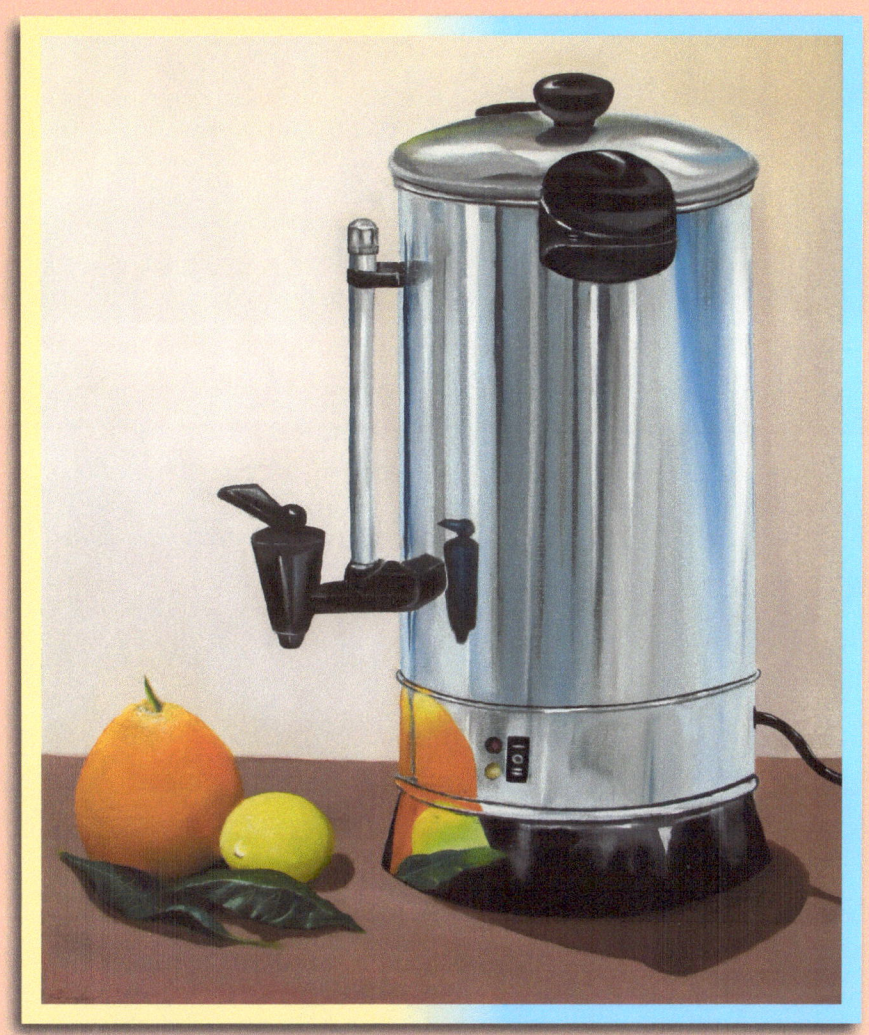
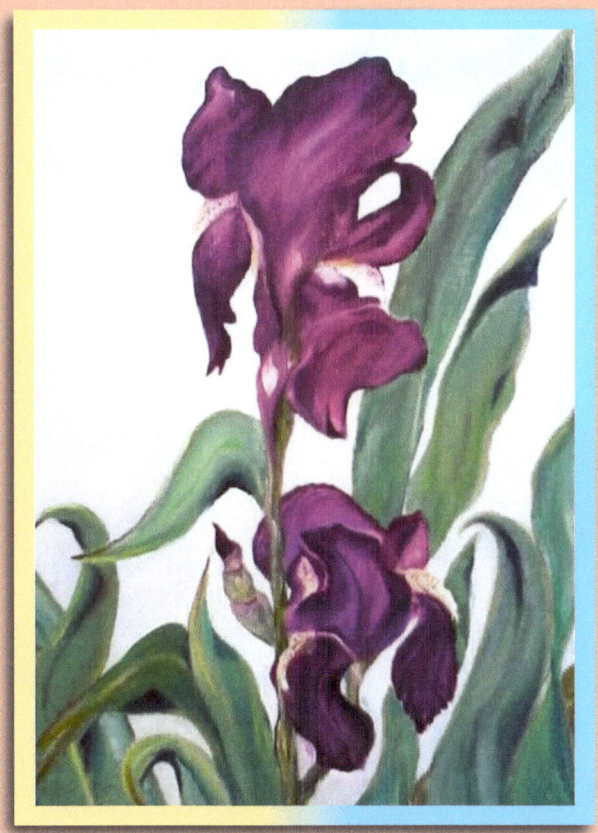
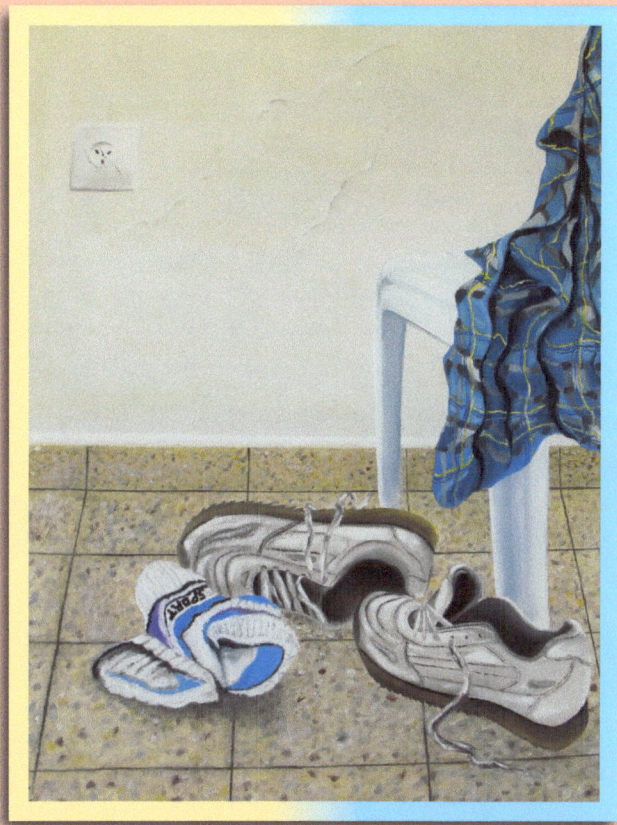

Dalia Rotem

- Painting
- dalia.rotem.art@gmail.com

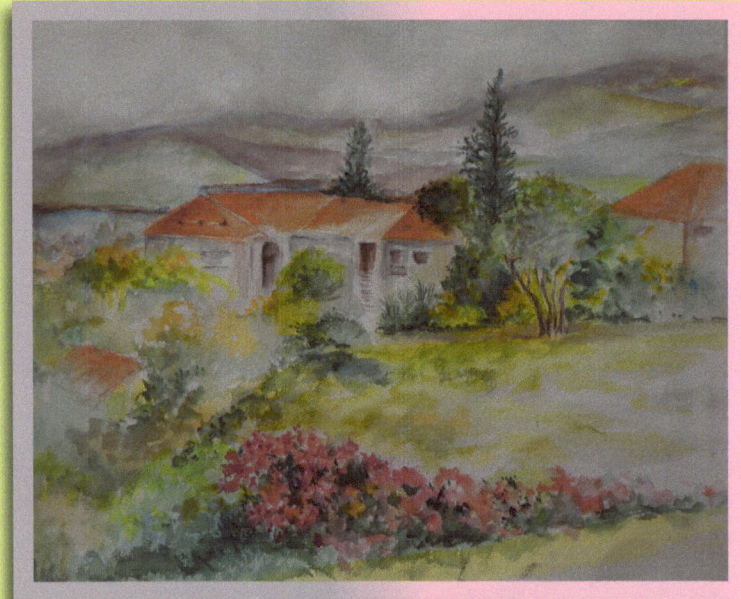
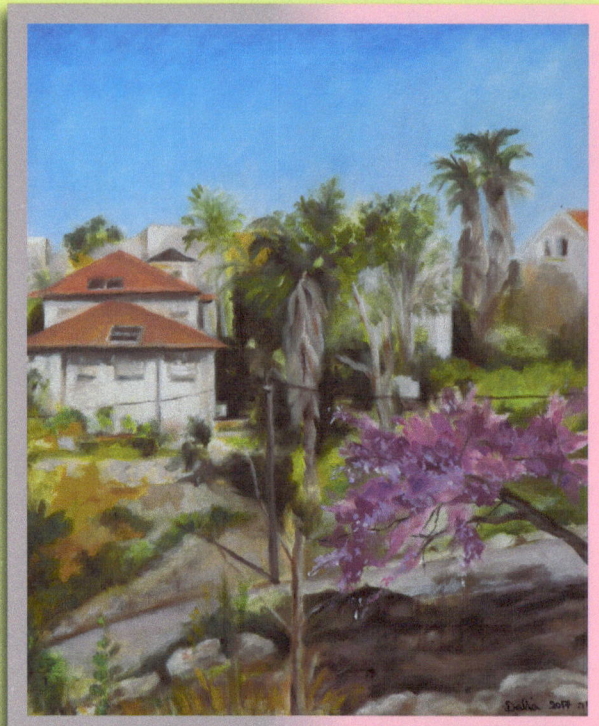

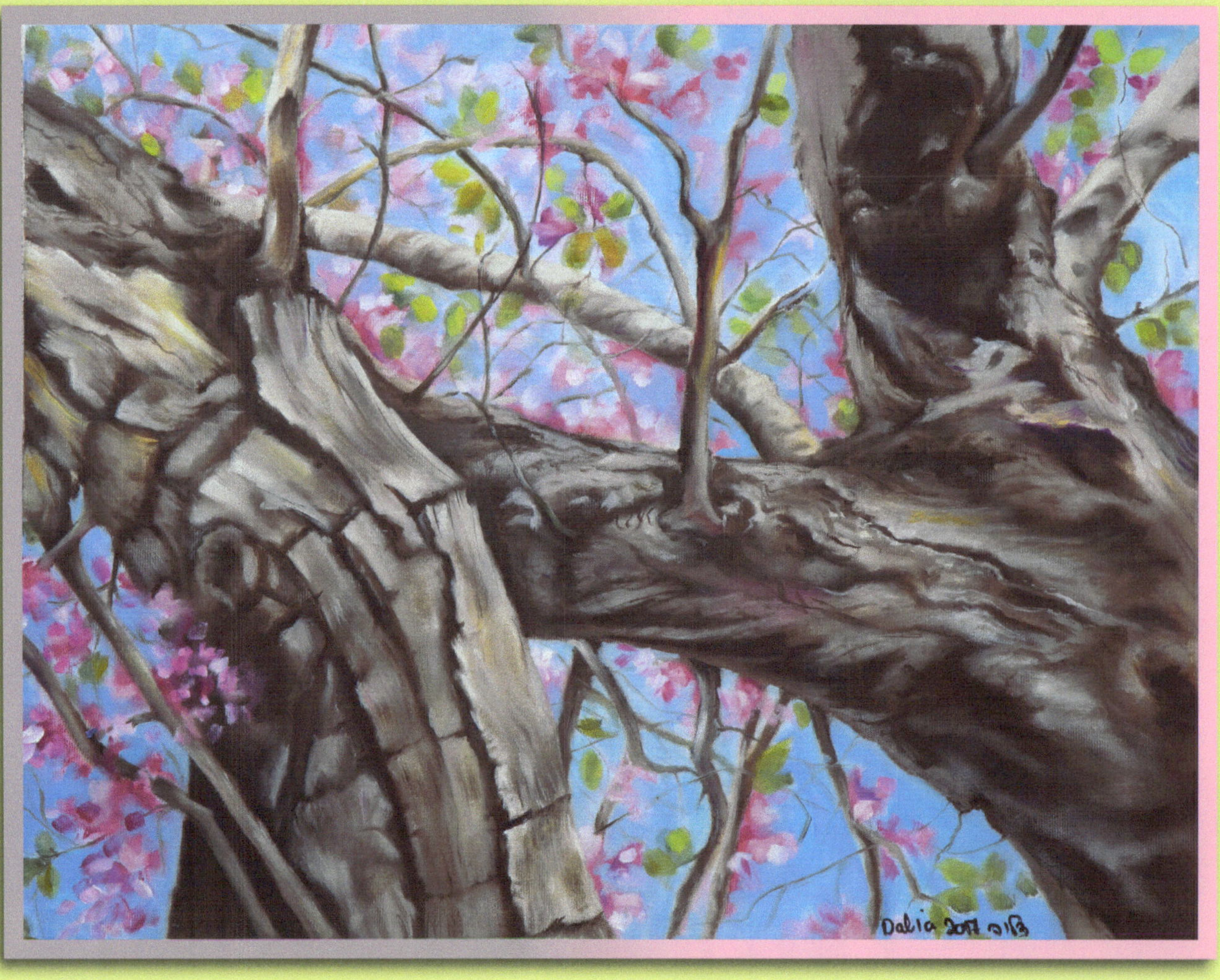

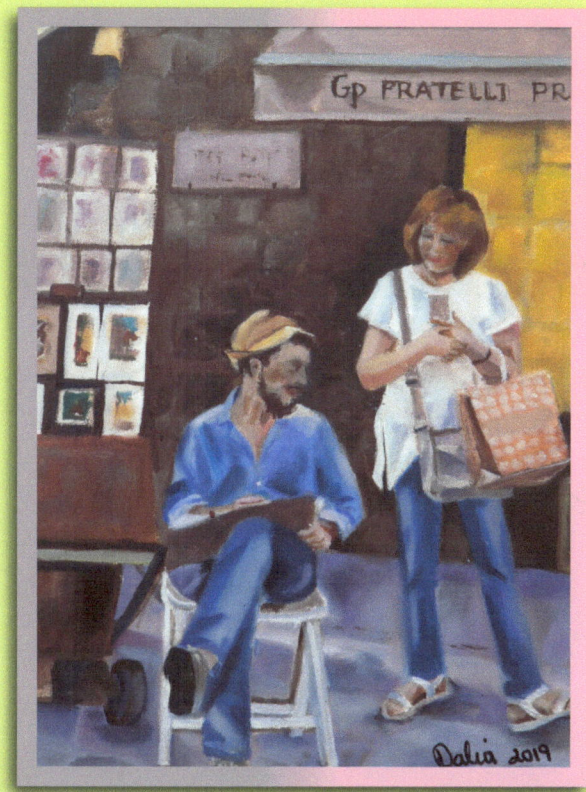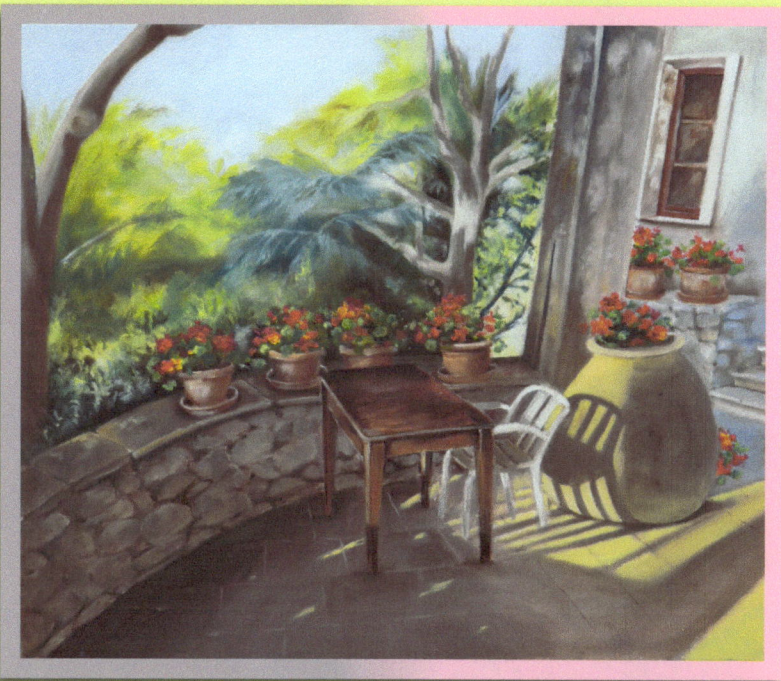

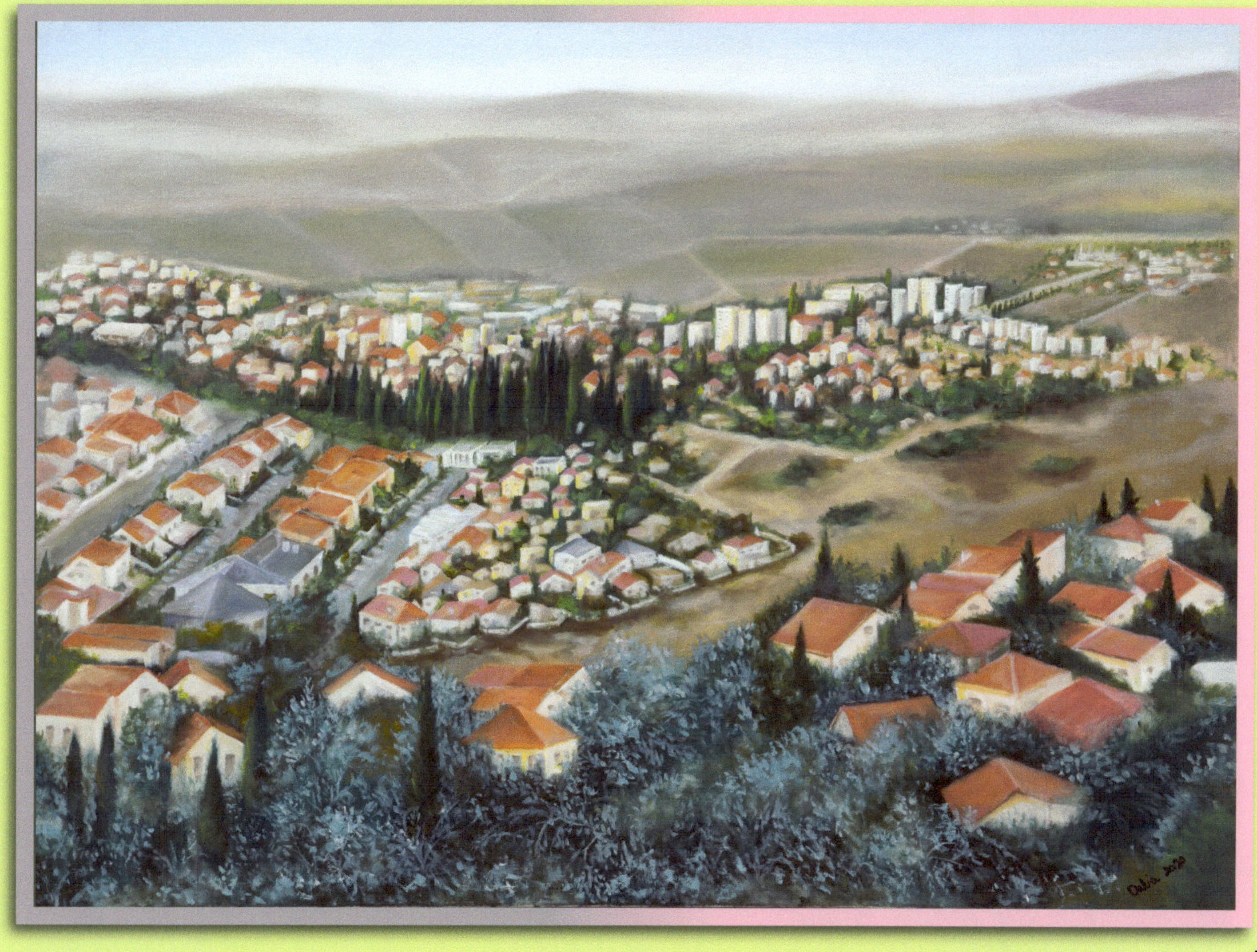

Yakov Korenblum

- Photography
- jacoko11@gmail.com
- Facebook: korenblum yakov

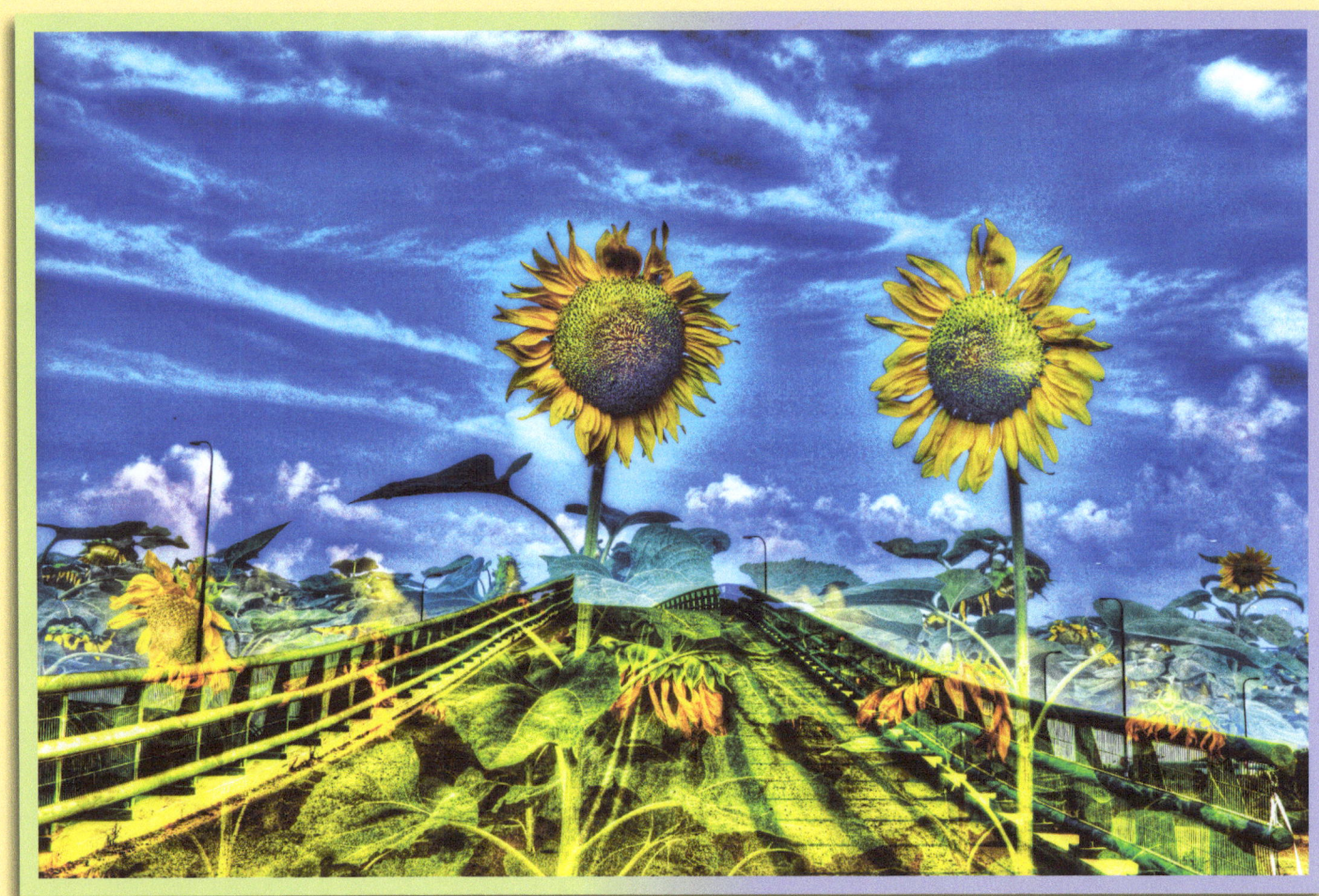

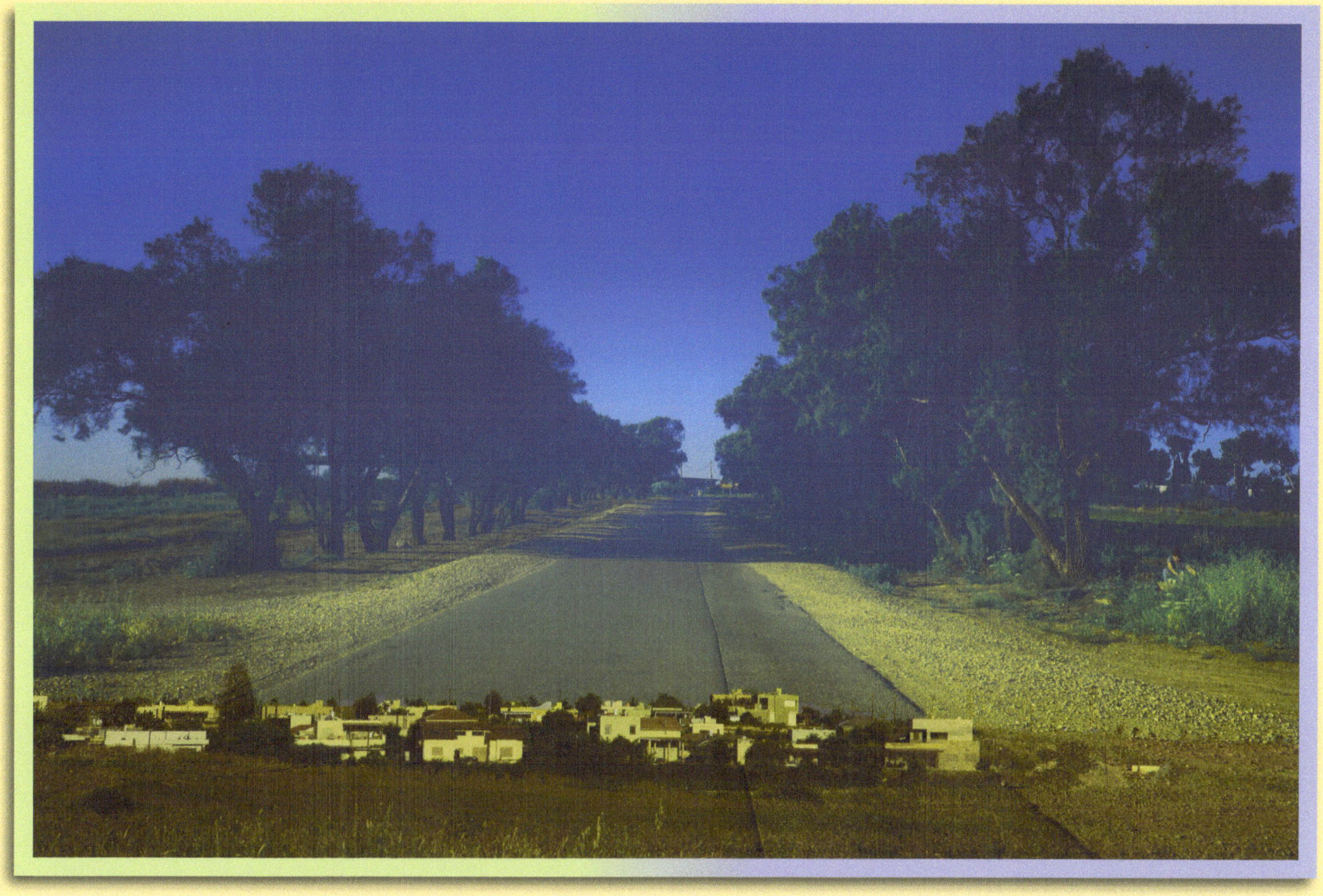

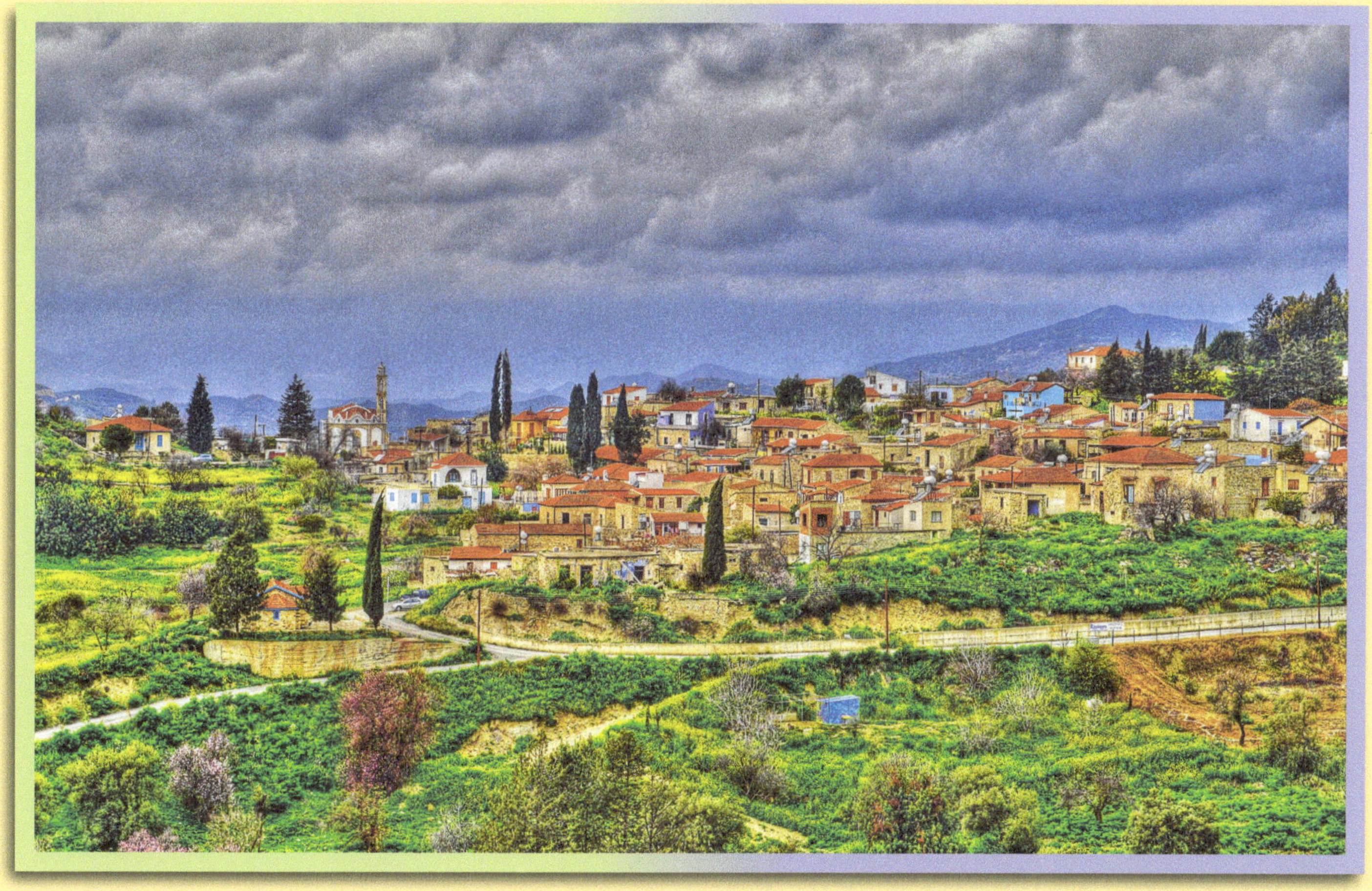

Dorit Amit

- Painting
- doritart@amitda.com
- http://doritamit.com

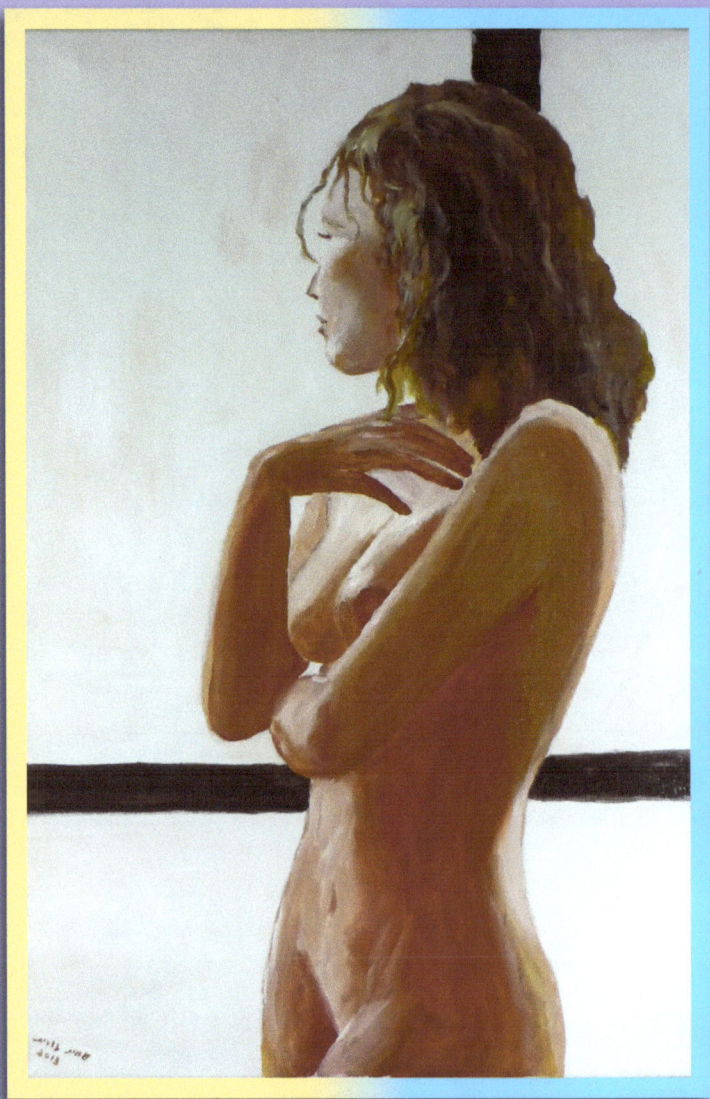

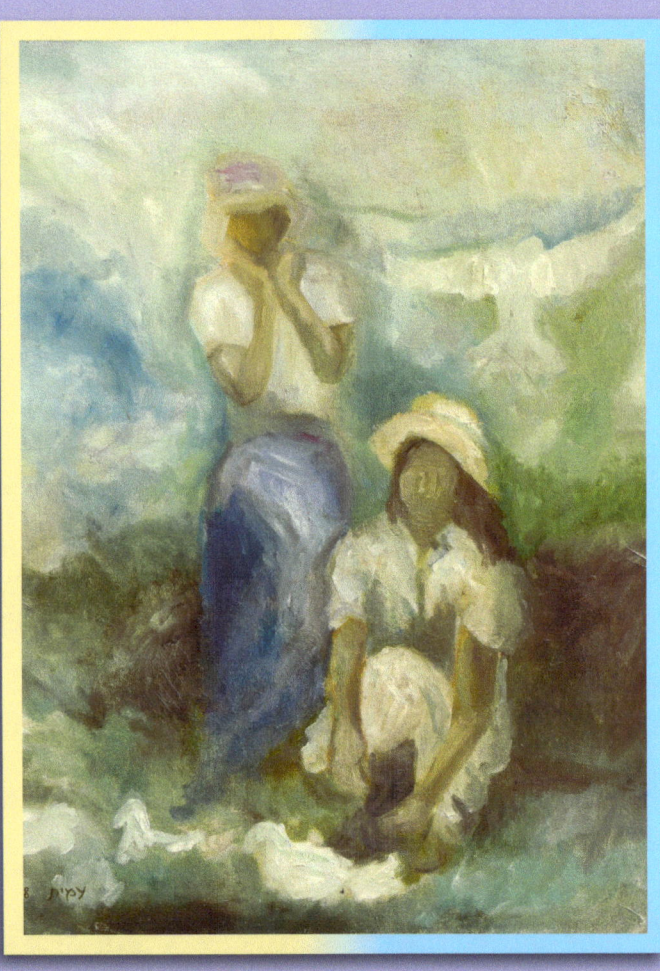

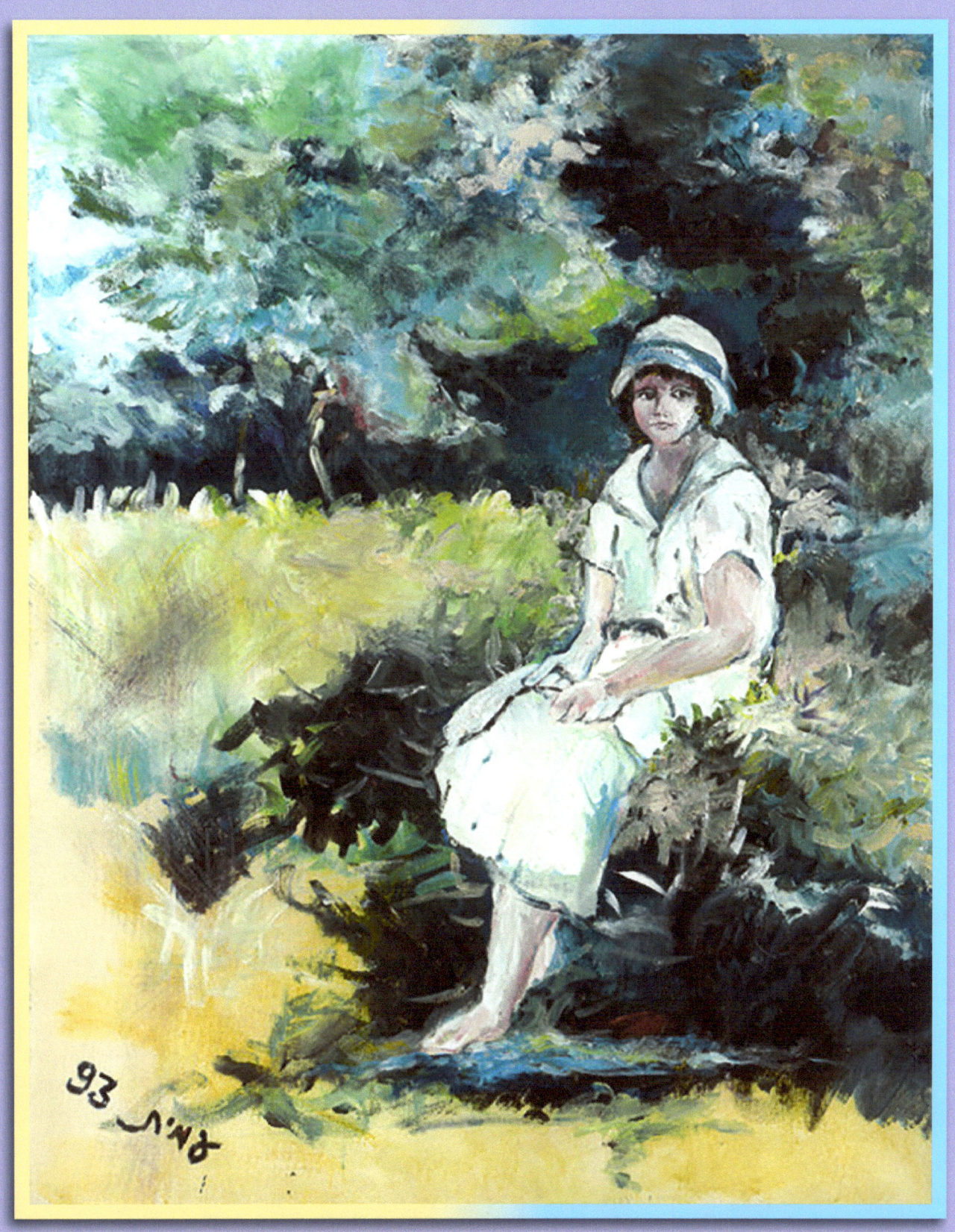

Michal Agmon Gonnen

✺ Photography
✺ michalbm@netvision.net.il
✺ www.facebook.com/womenworkphoto
✺ www.instagram.com/Womenworkphoto

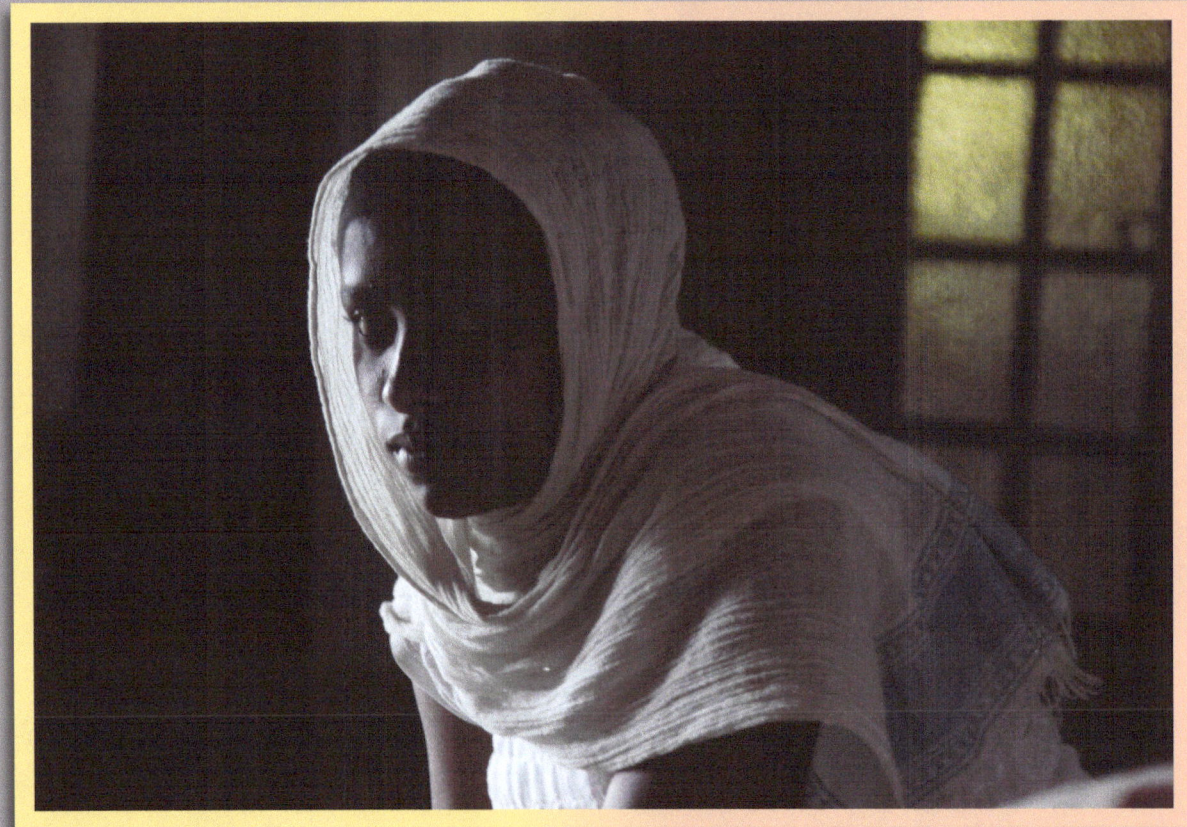

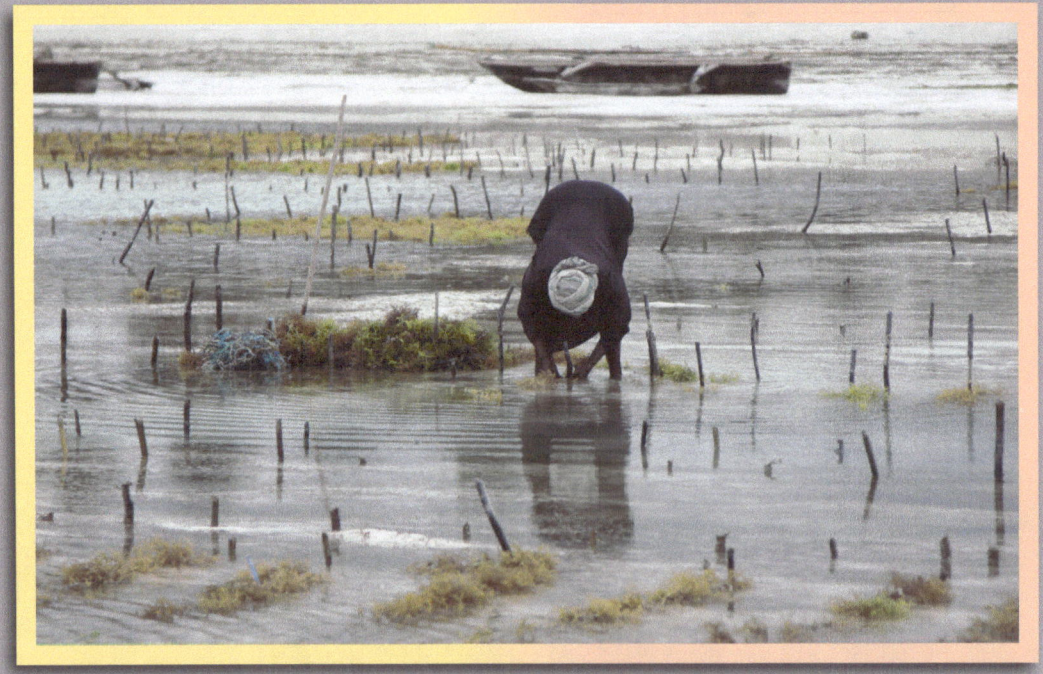

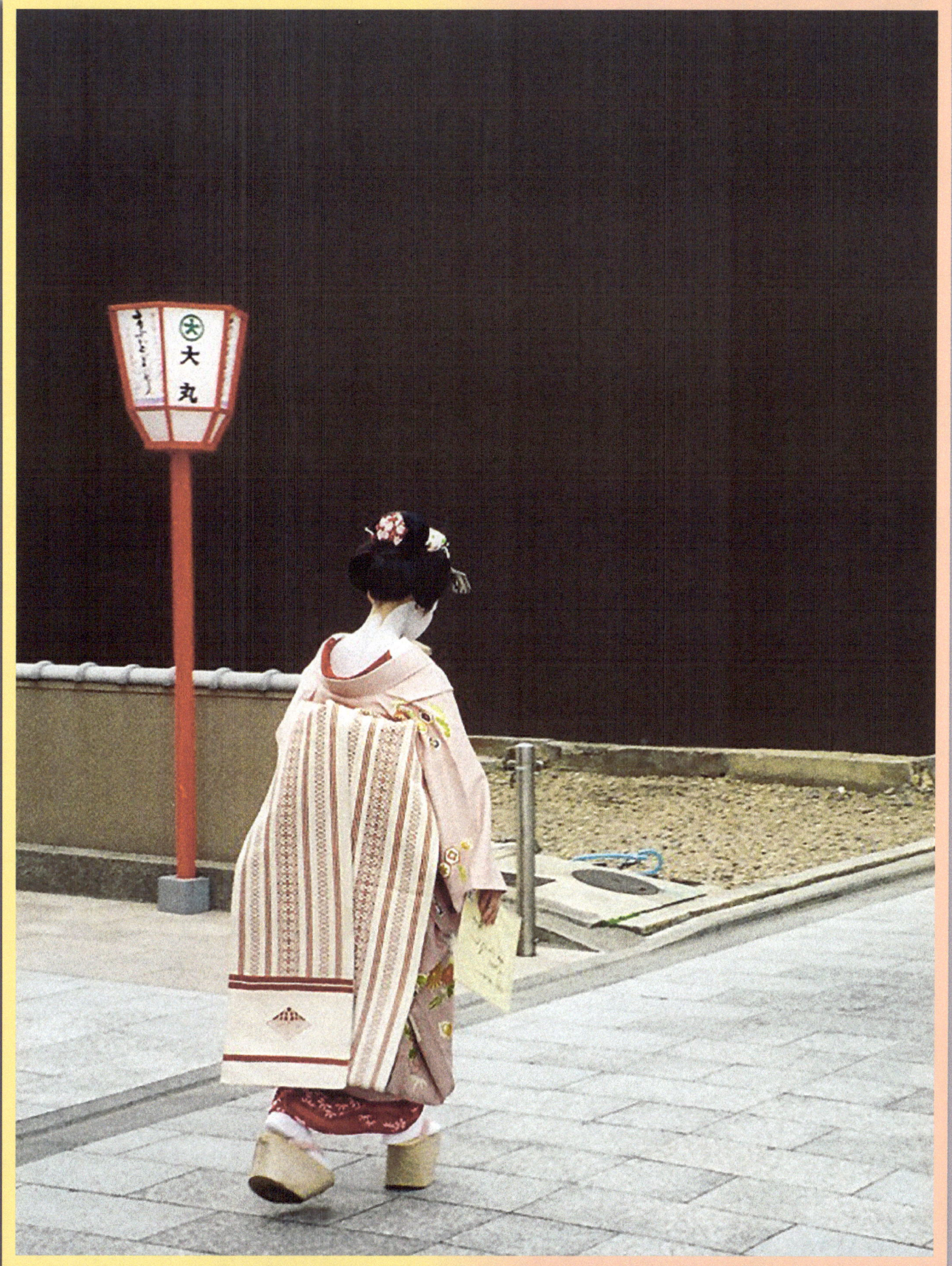

Shay Aloni

- Photography
- alonishay@gmail.com
- shayaloni.co.il

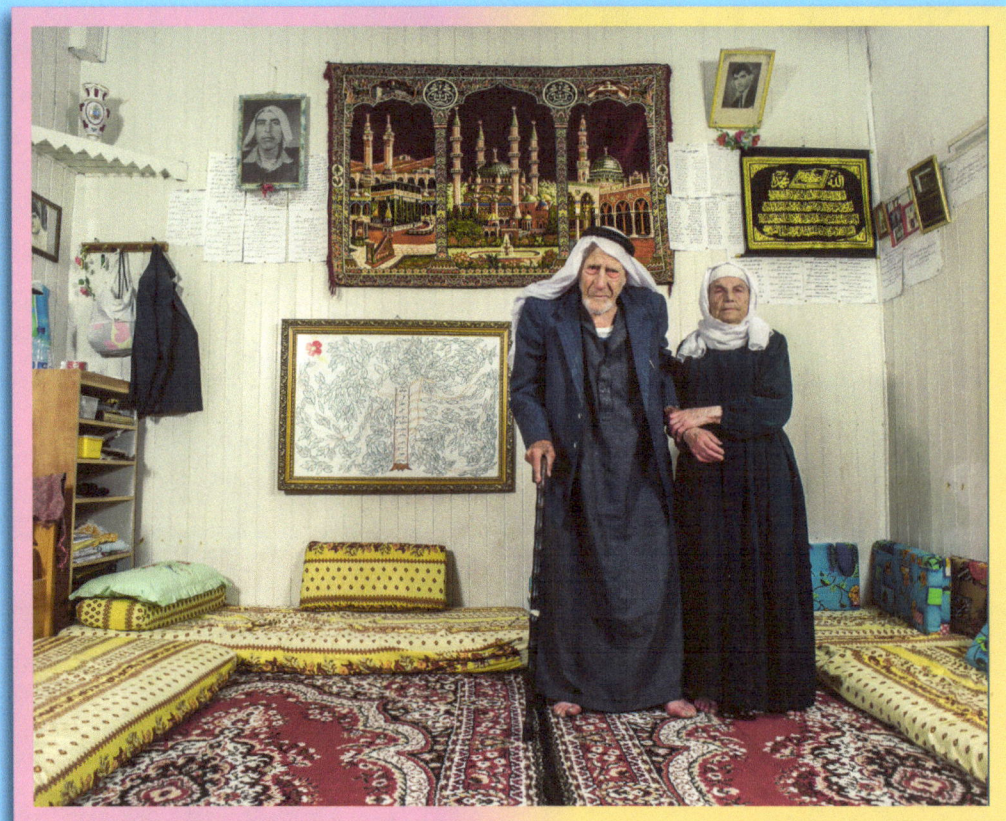

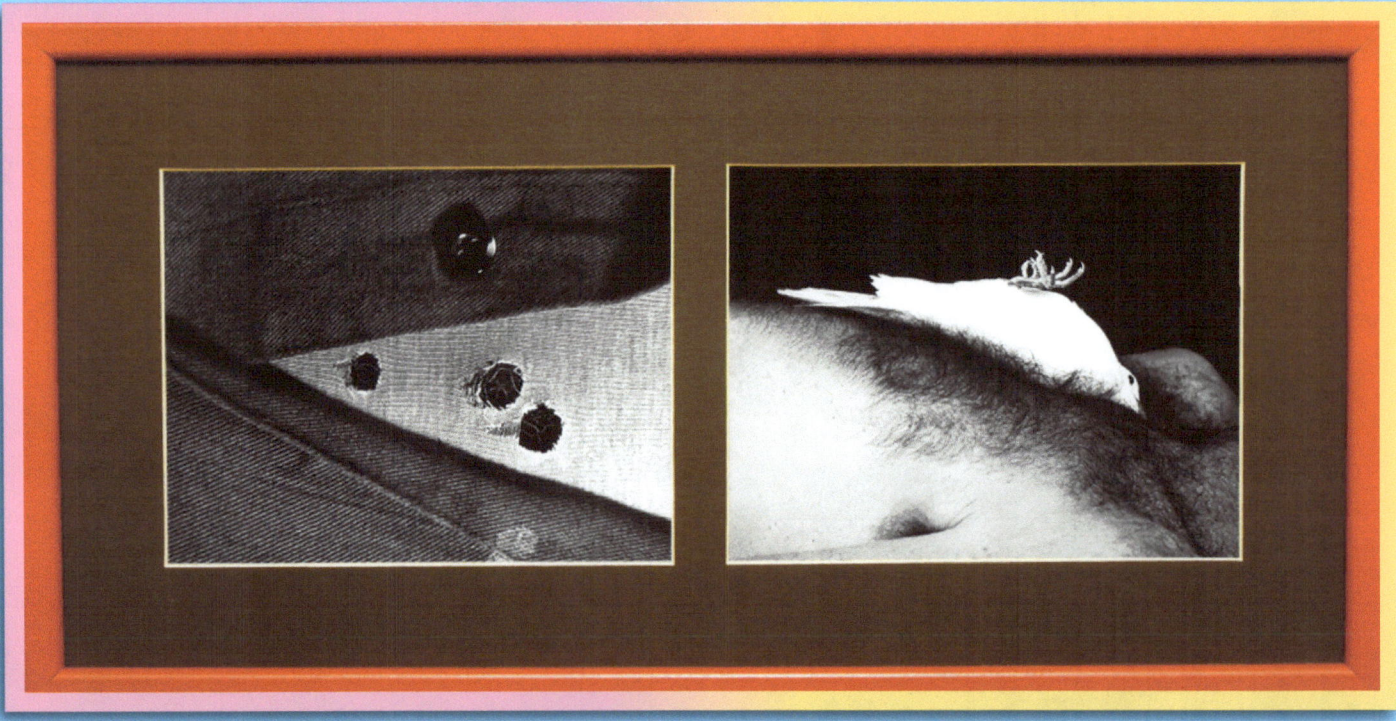

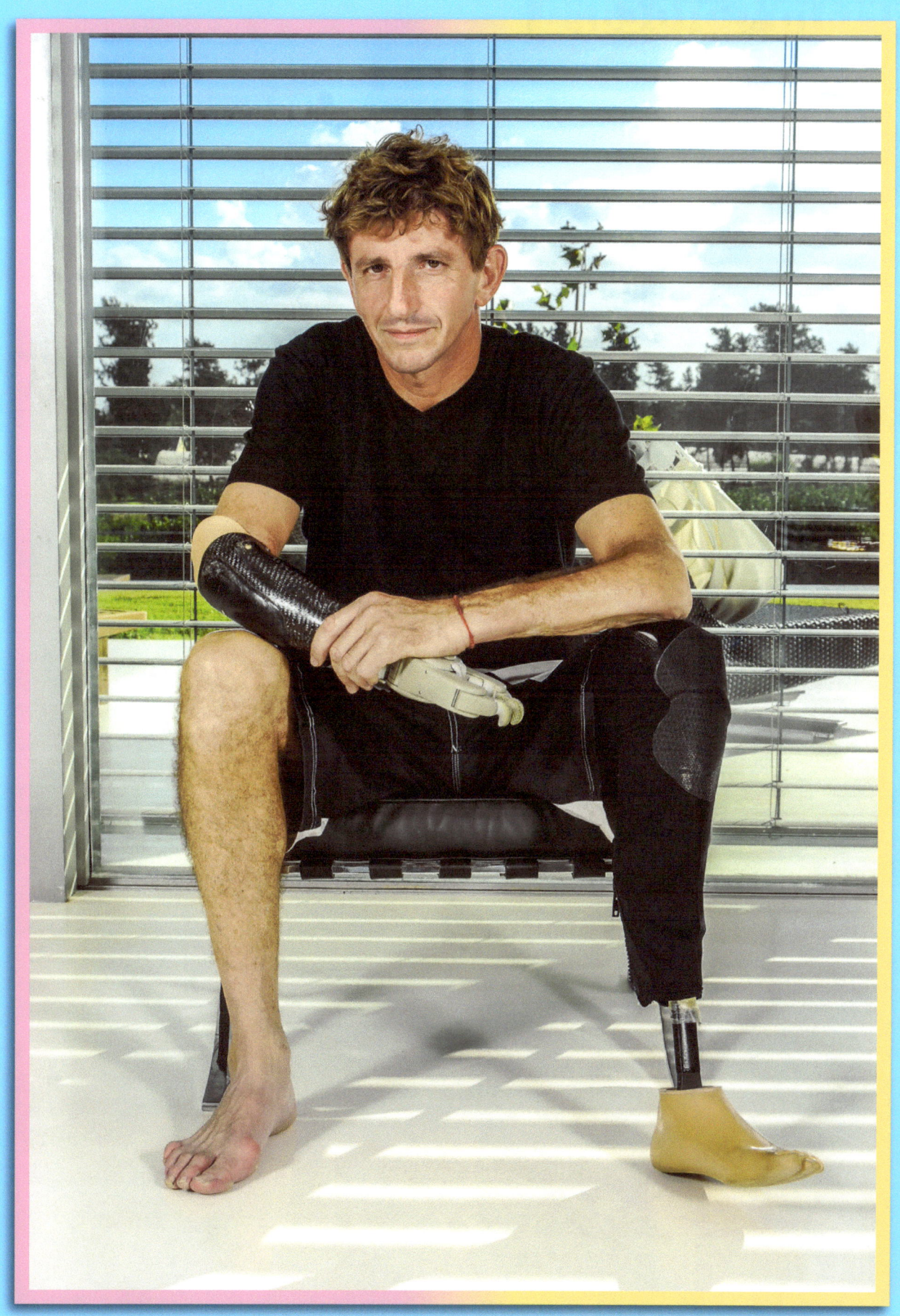

Miriam Cojocaru

- Painting
- Miriam.Cojocaru@biu.ac.il

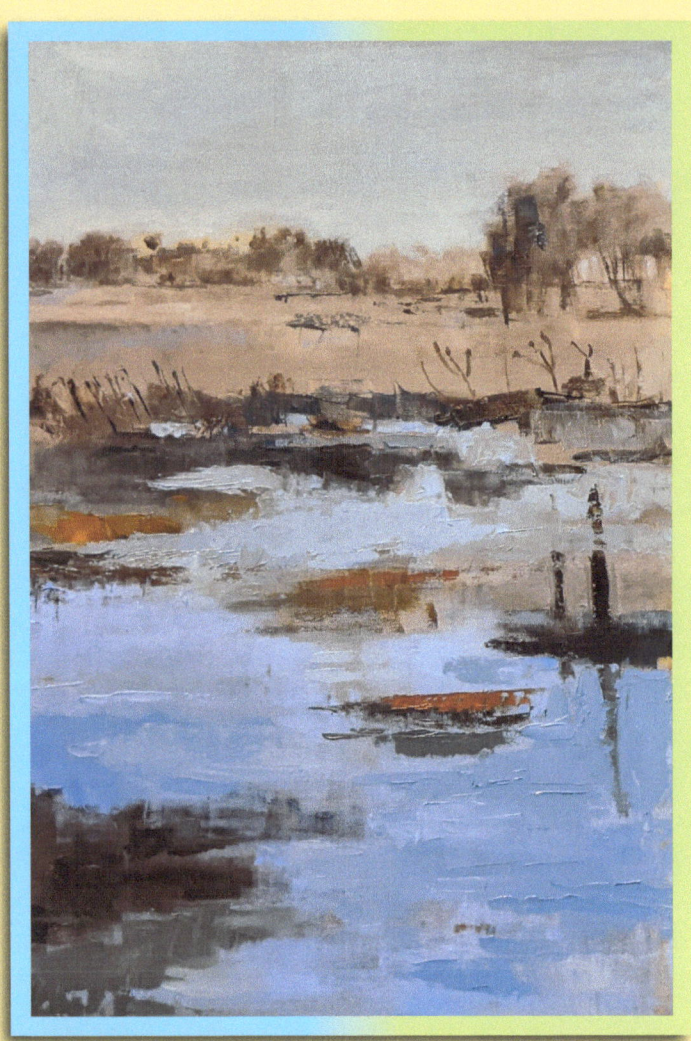
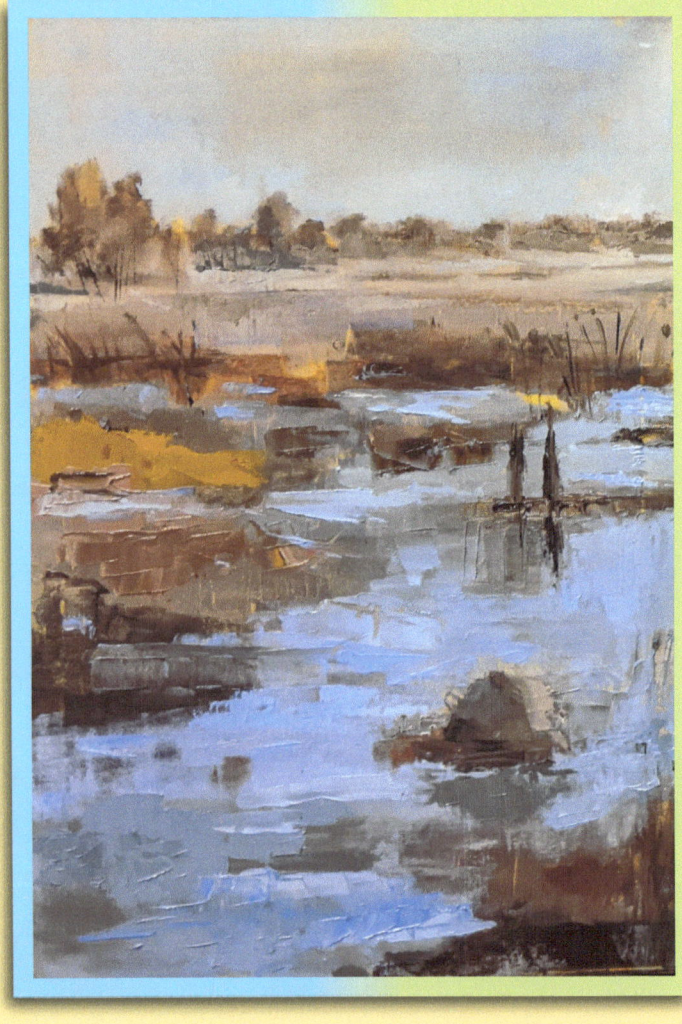

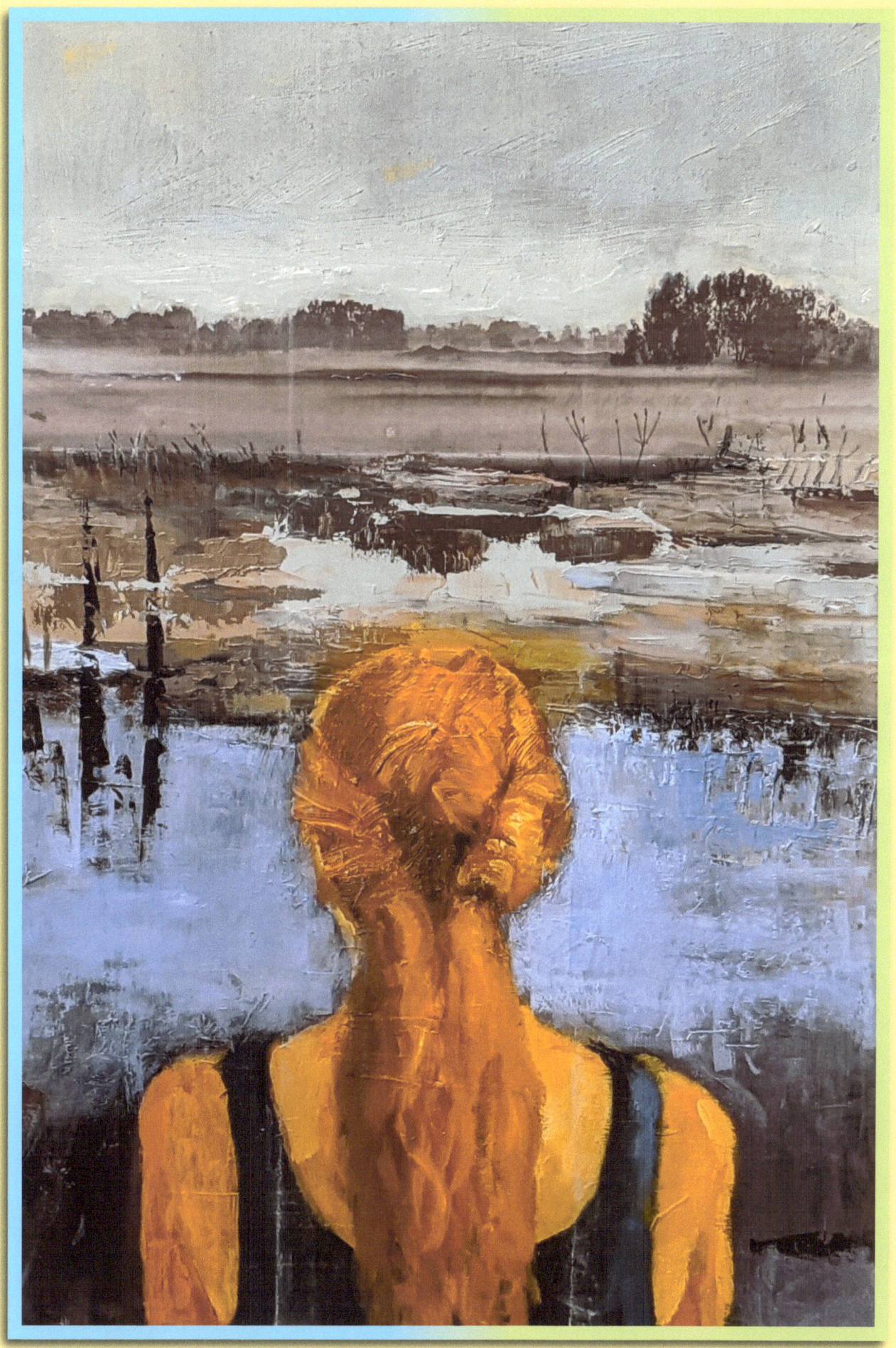

Yair David

- **Watercolors Painting**
- yair@davidart.co.il
- davidart.co.il

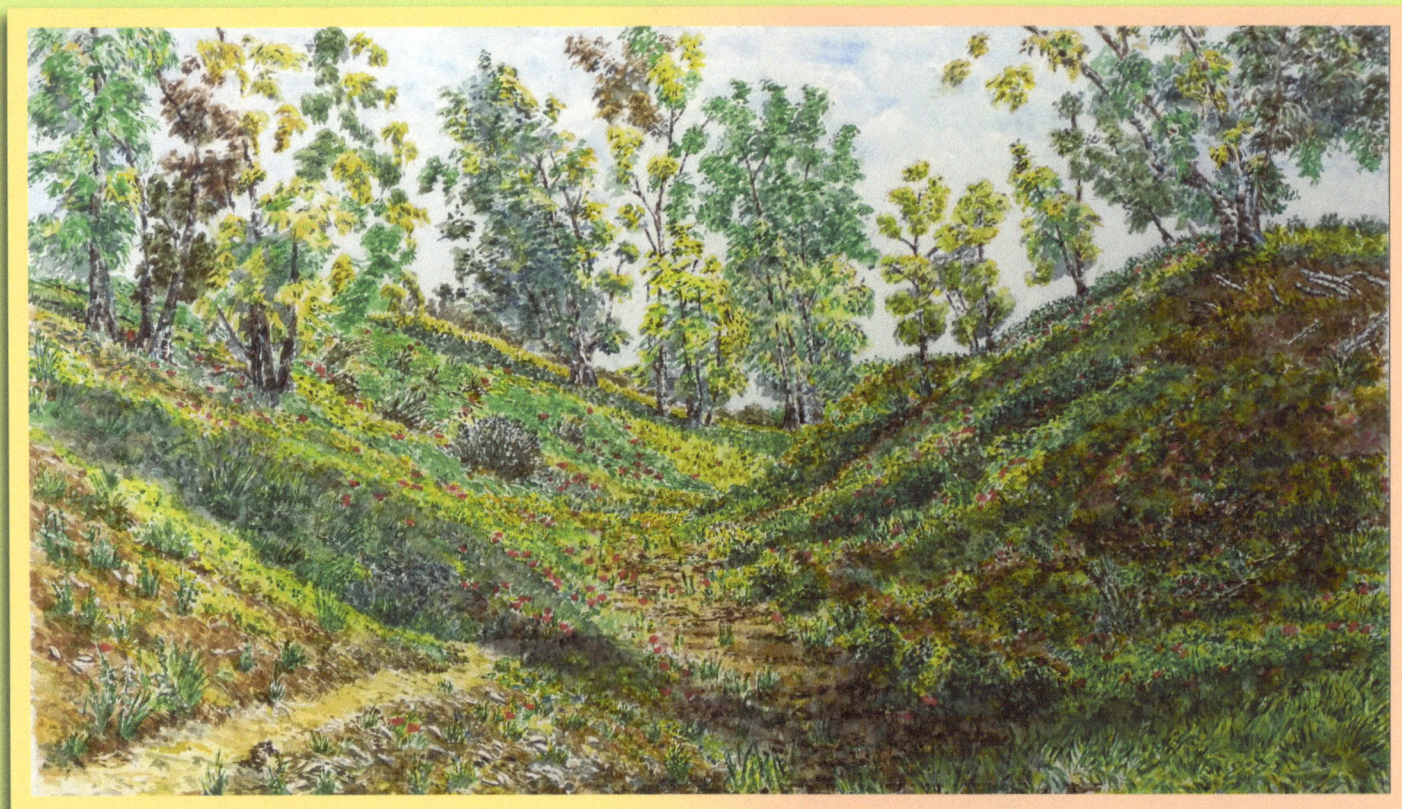

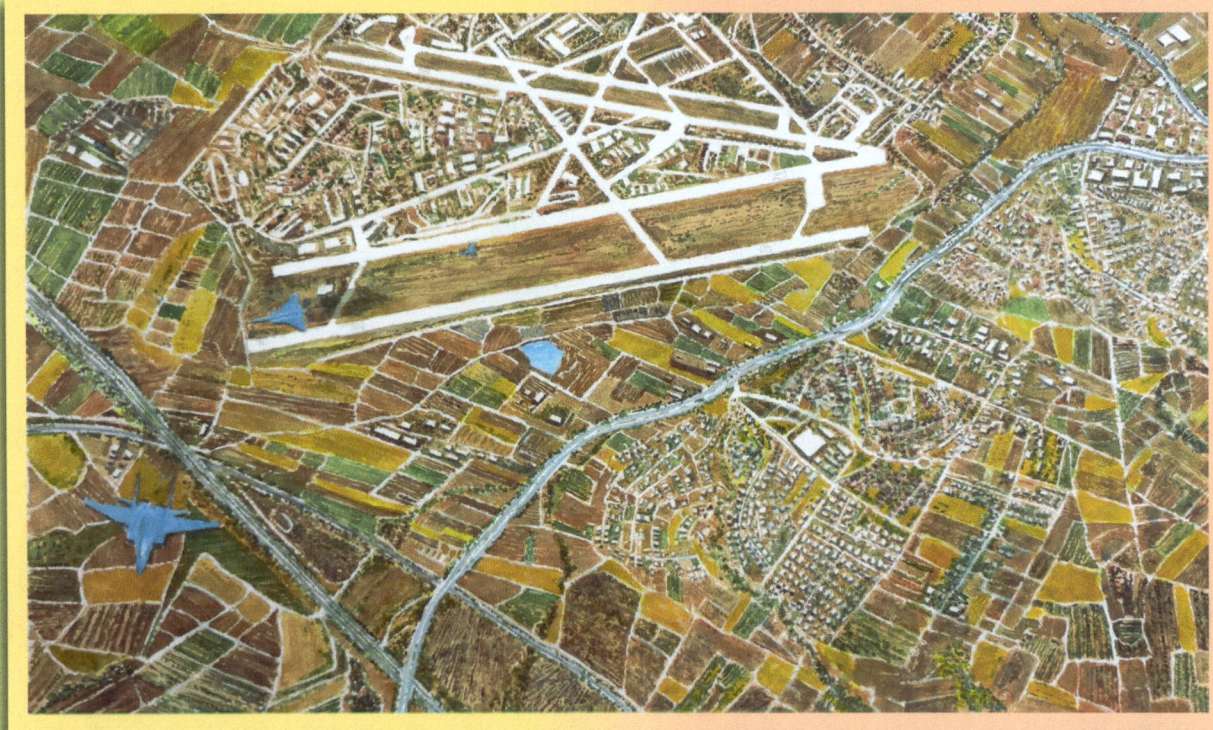

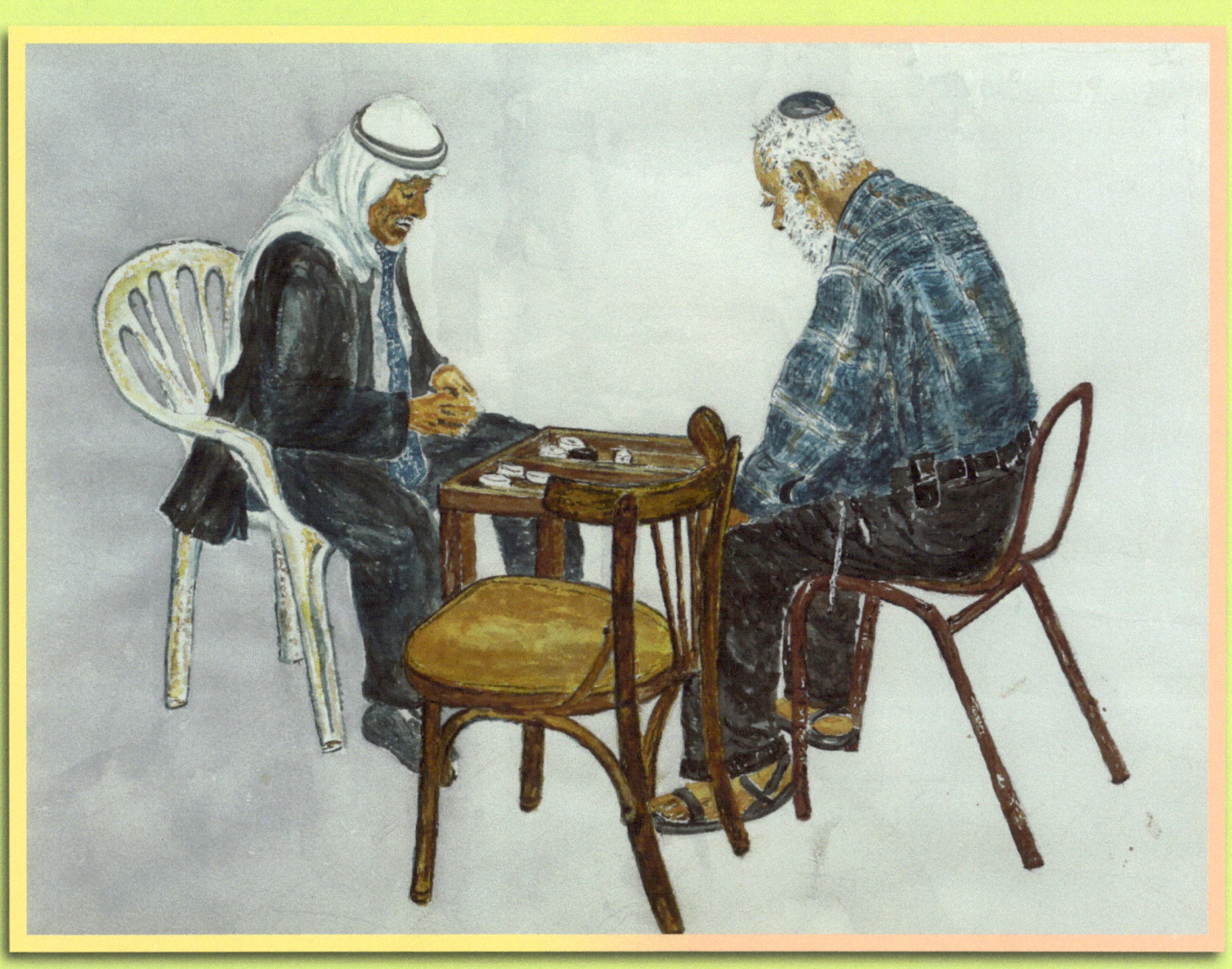

Shlomo Emanuel

- Painting and Sculpture
- shlomoe@atlasct.com
- www.emanueliart.com
- instagram: emanuelshlomo
- facebook: Shlomo Emanuel

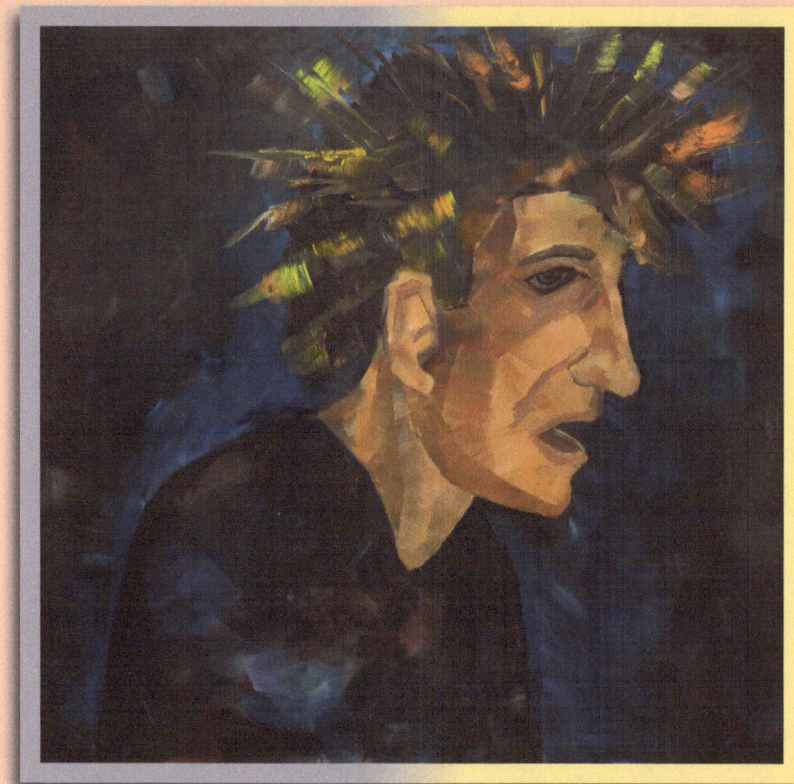

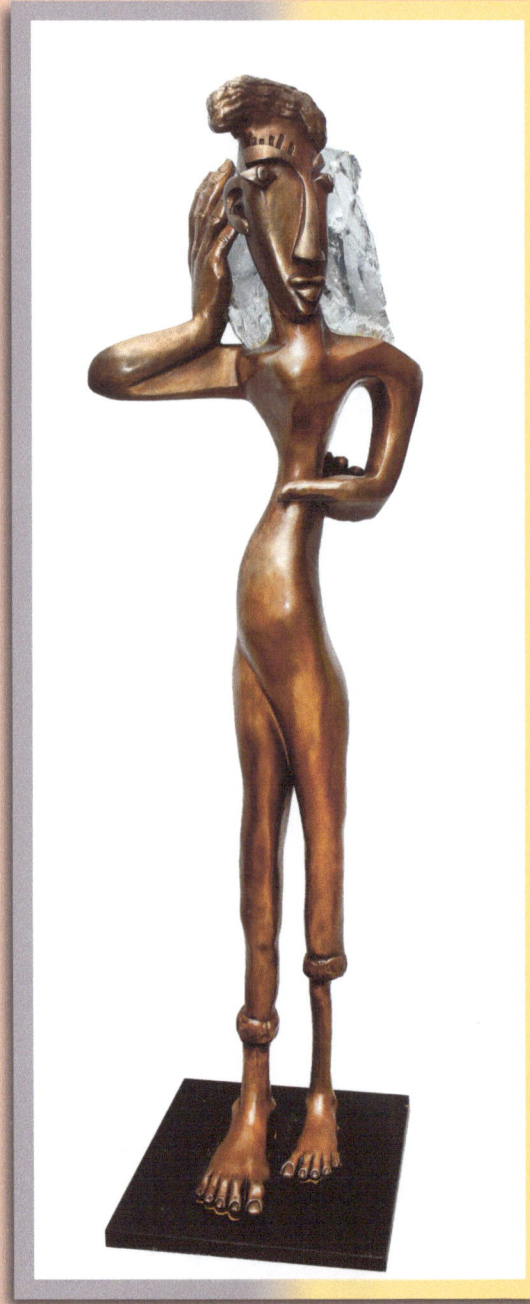

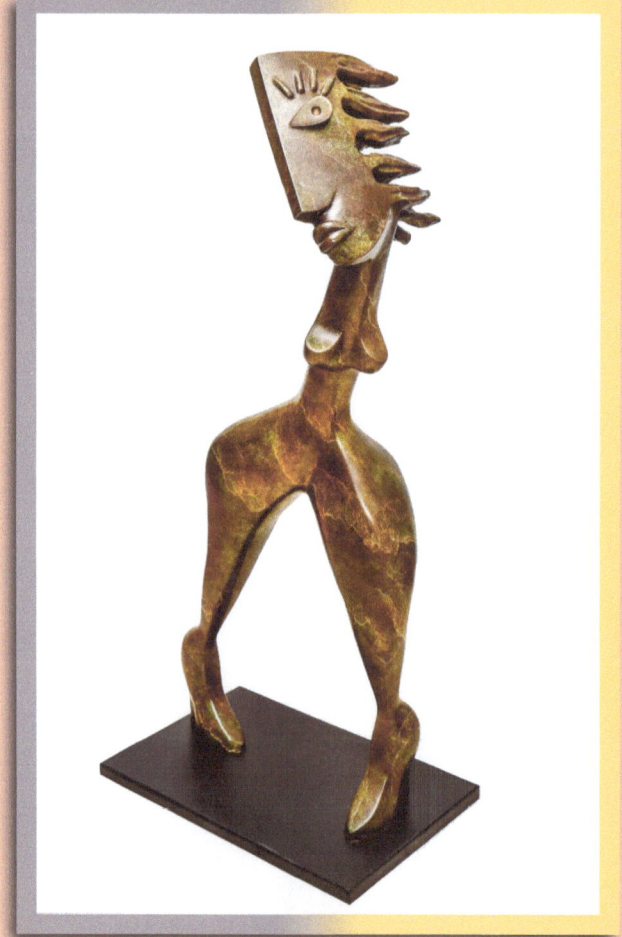

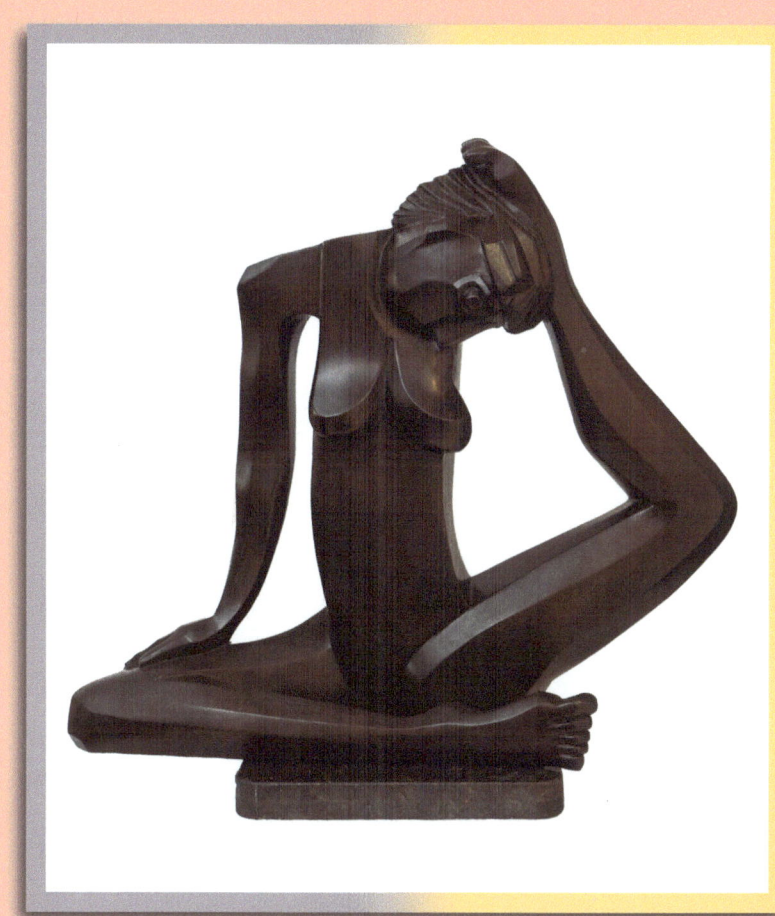
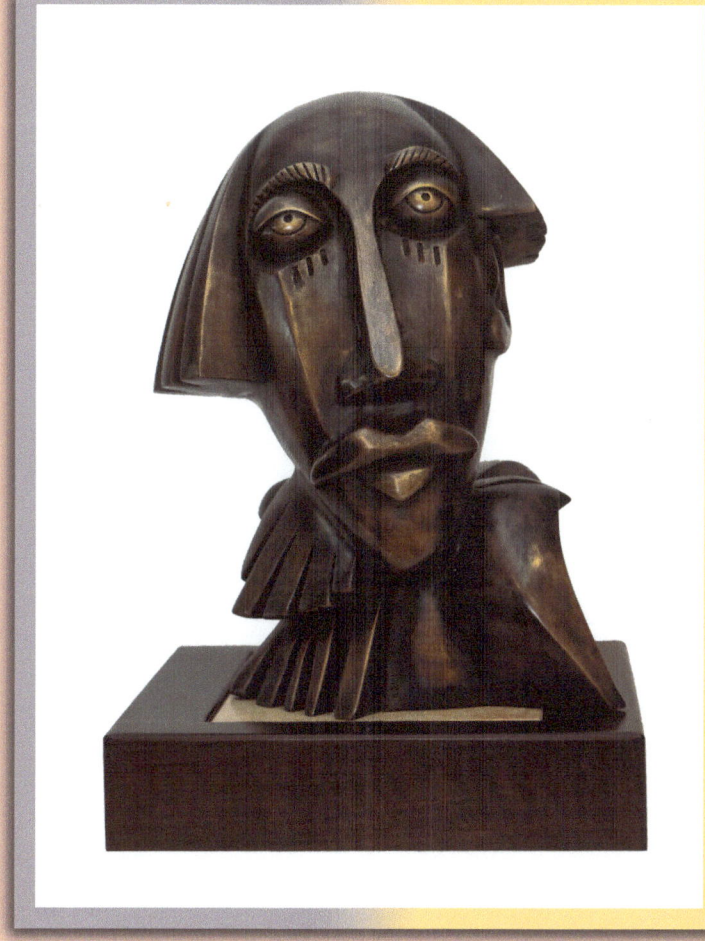
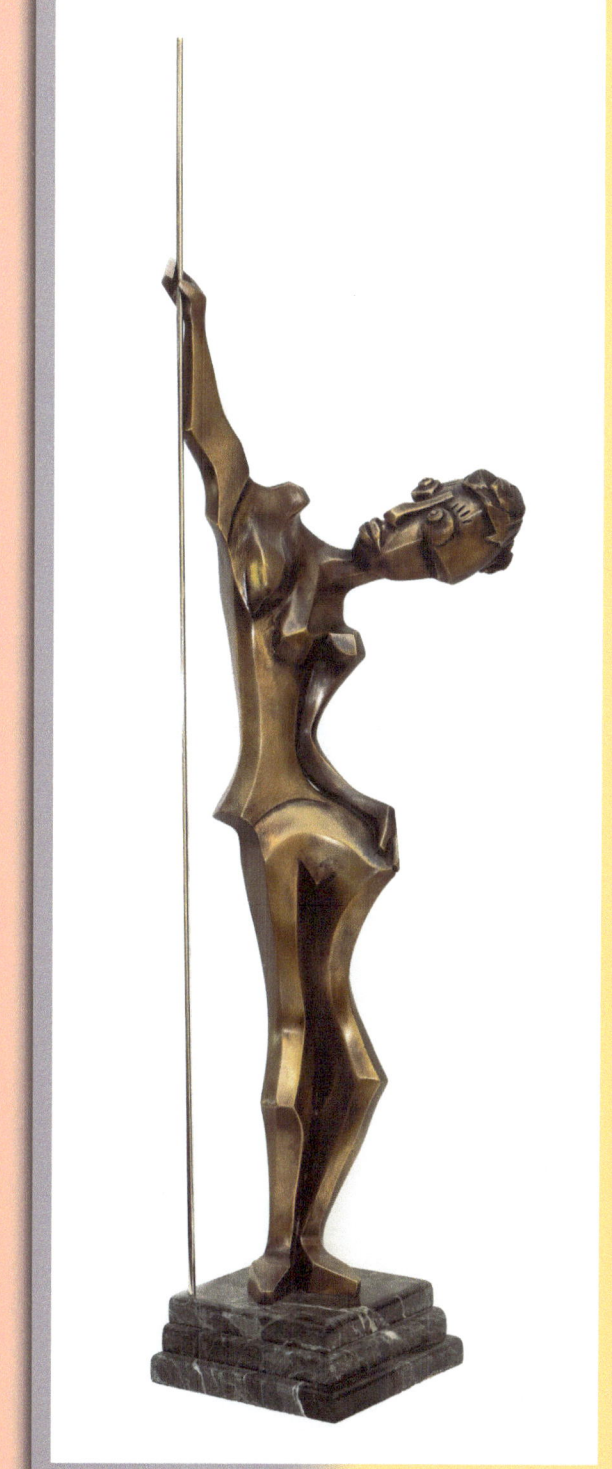

Ilan Goldstein

- Painting and drawing
- ilan.goldstein@gmail.com
- www.facebook.com/ilan.goldstein.5
- www.facebook.com/ilan.goldstein.6

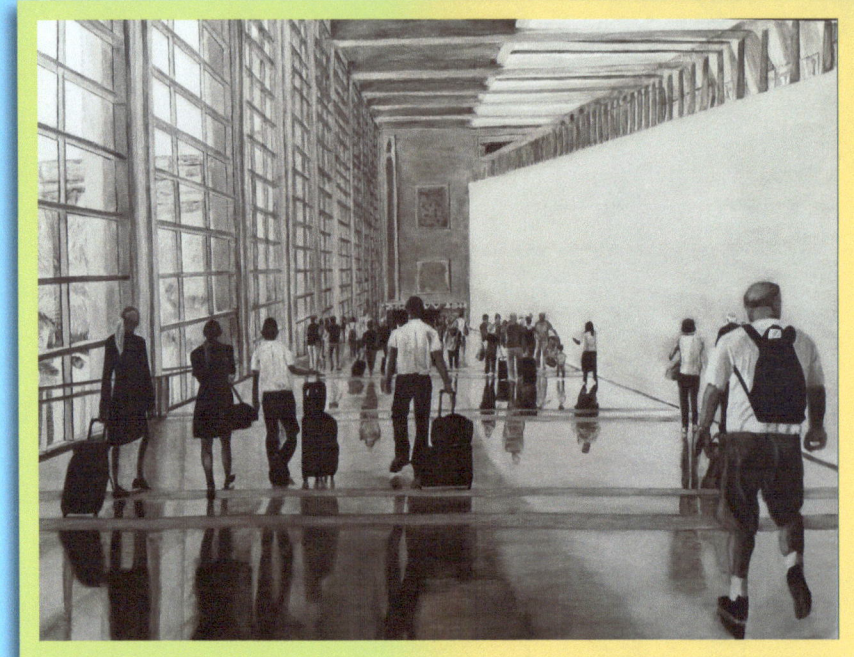

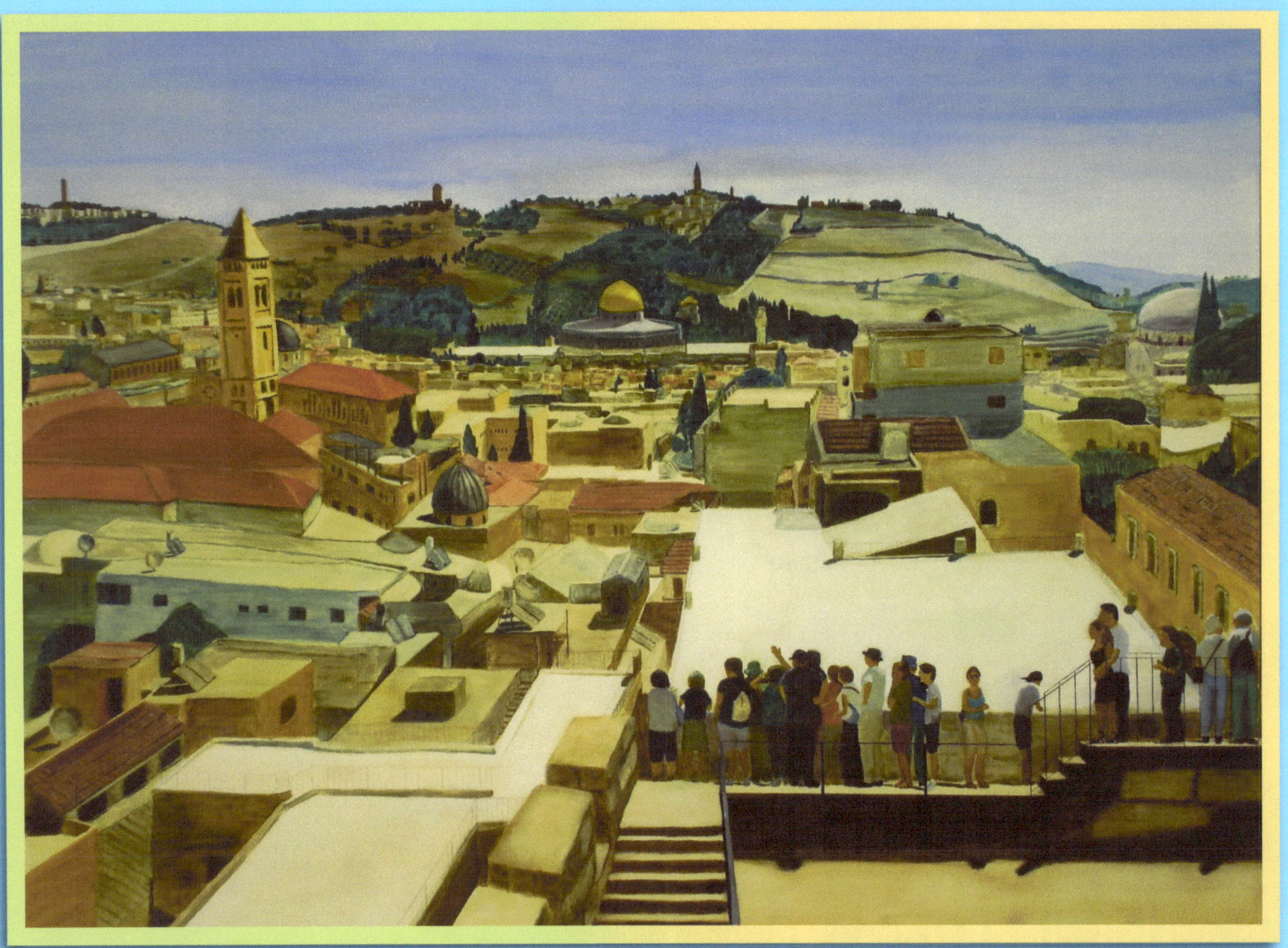

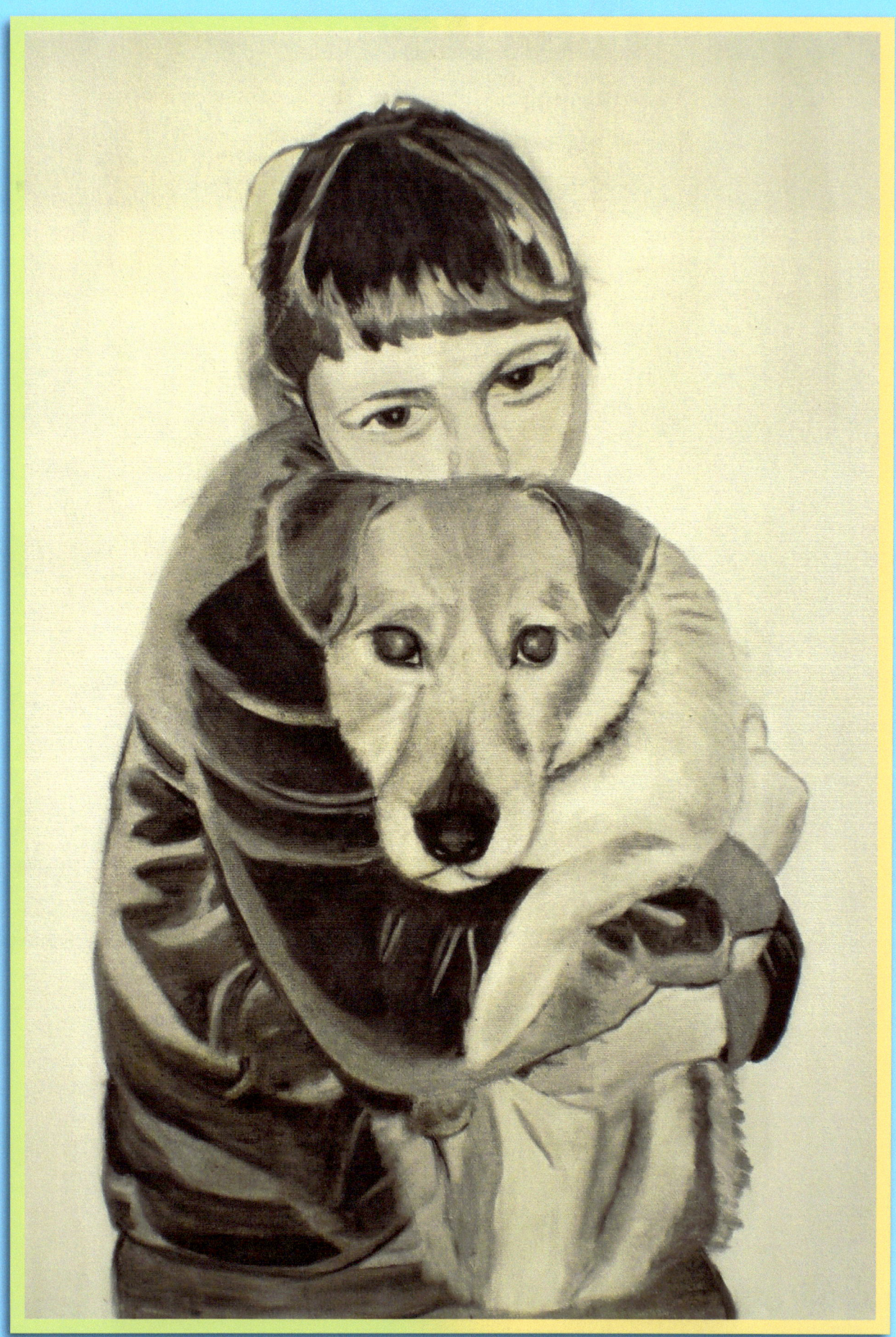

Michal Goren

✺ Painting
✺ mfgoren@gmail.com
✺ instagram: goren_michal

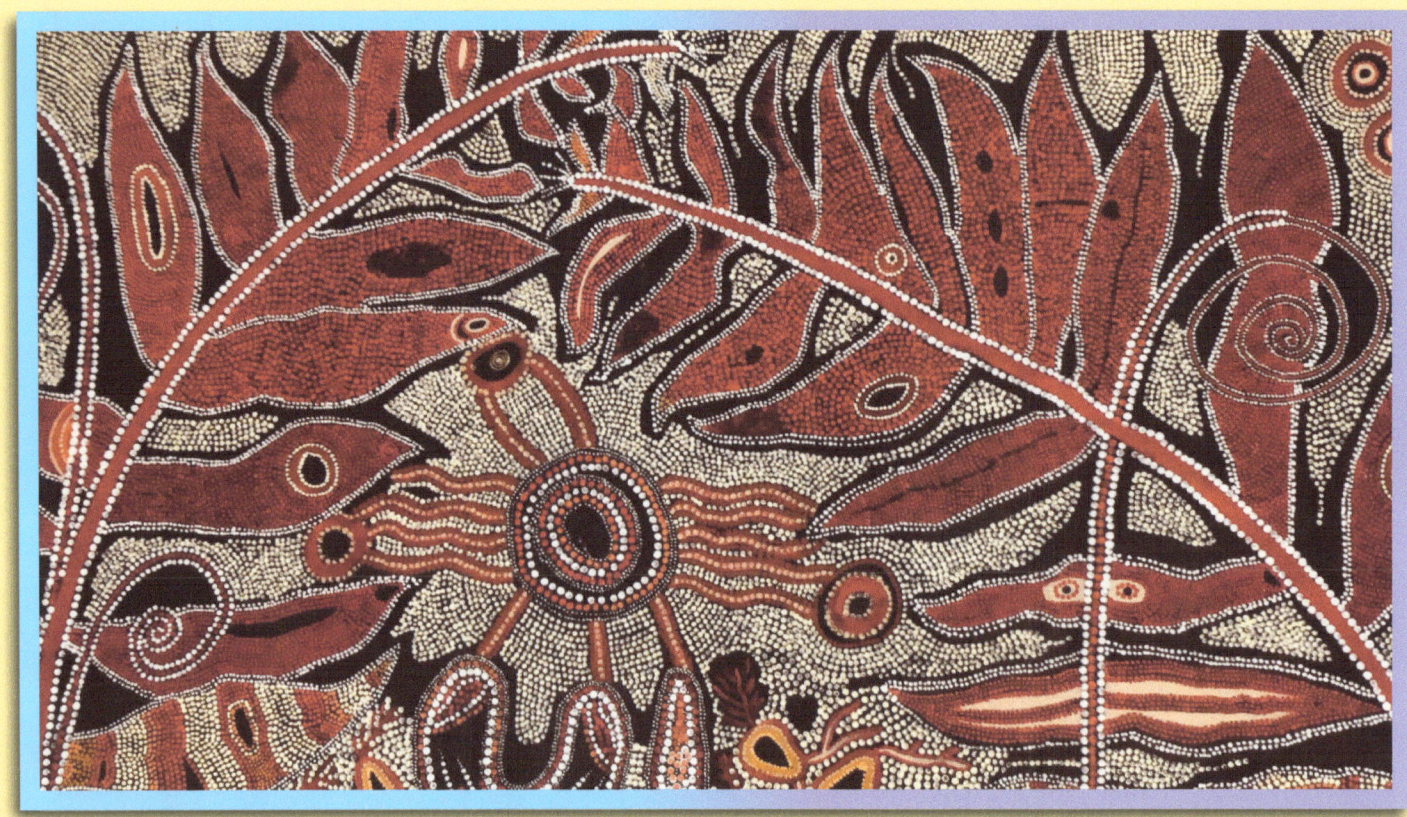

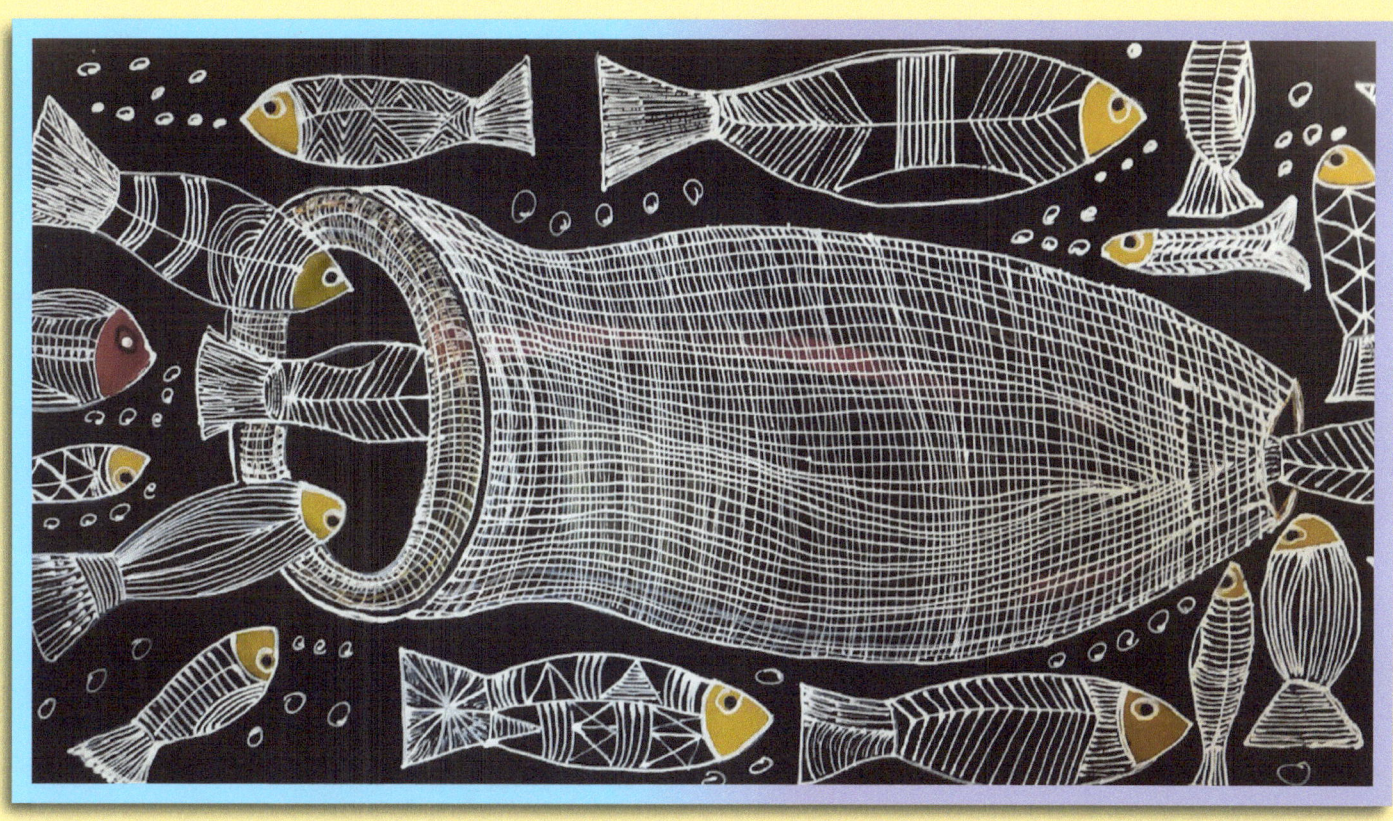
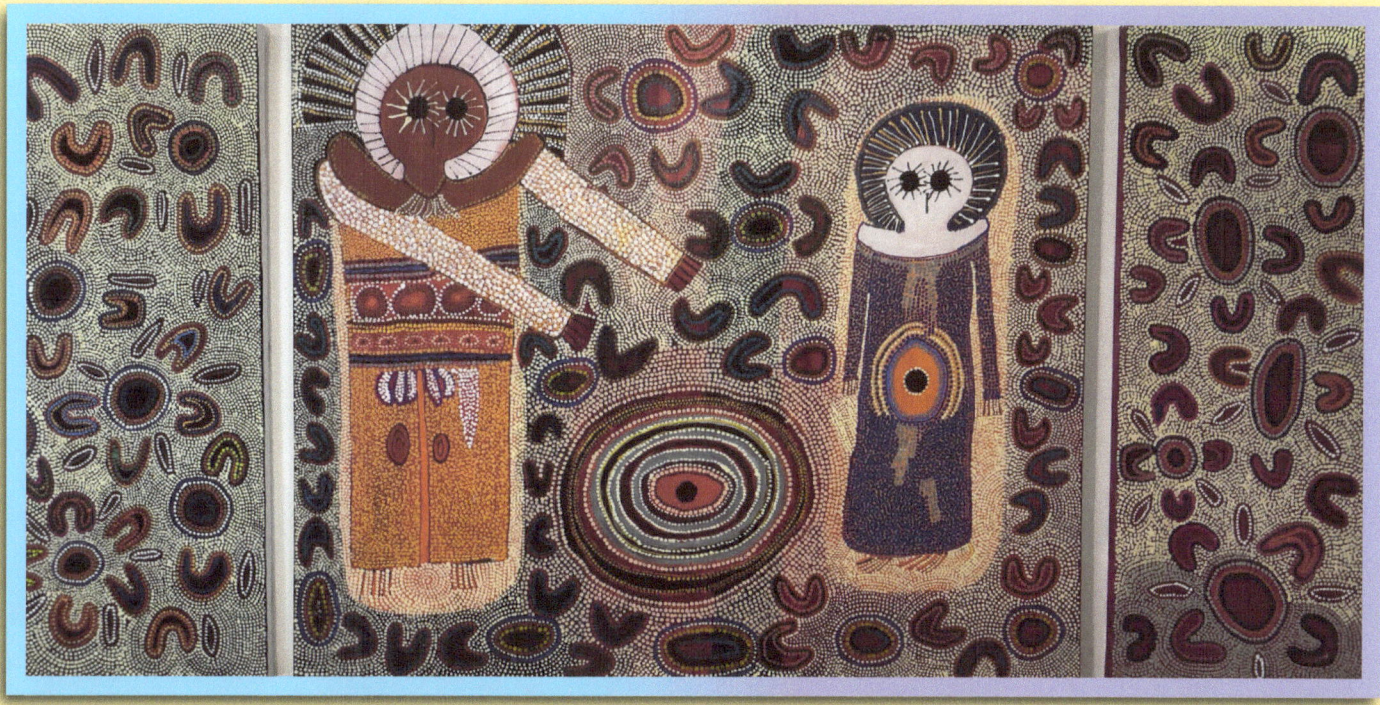

Irit Haskin

- Painting
- irithaskin@gmail.com
- facebook: Irena Haskin (Irit Haskin)

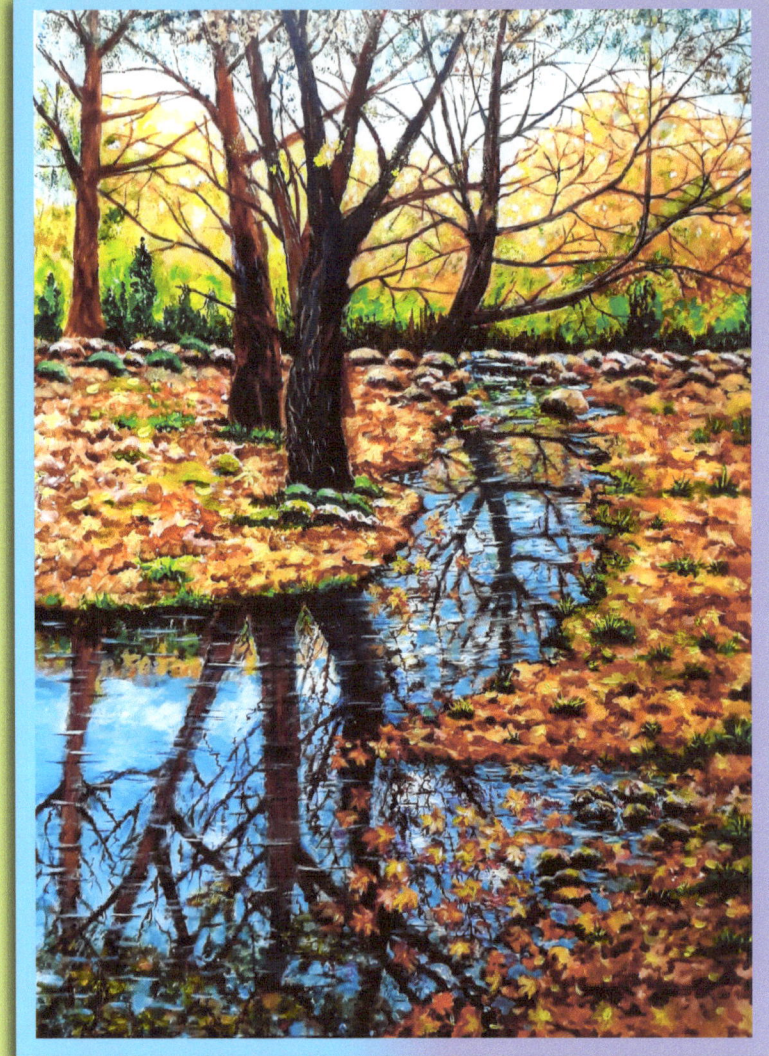

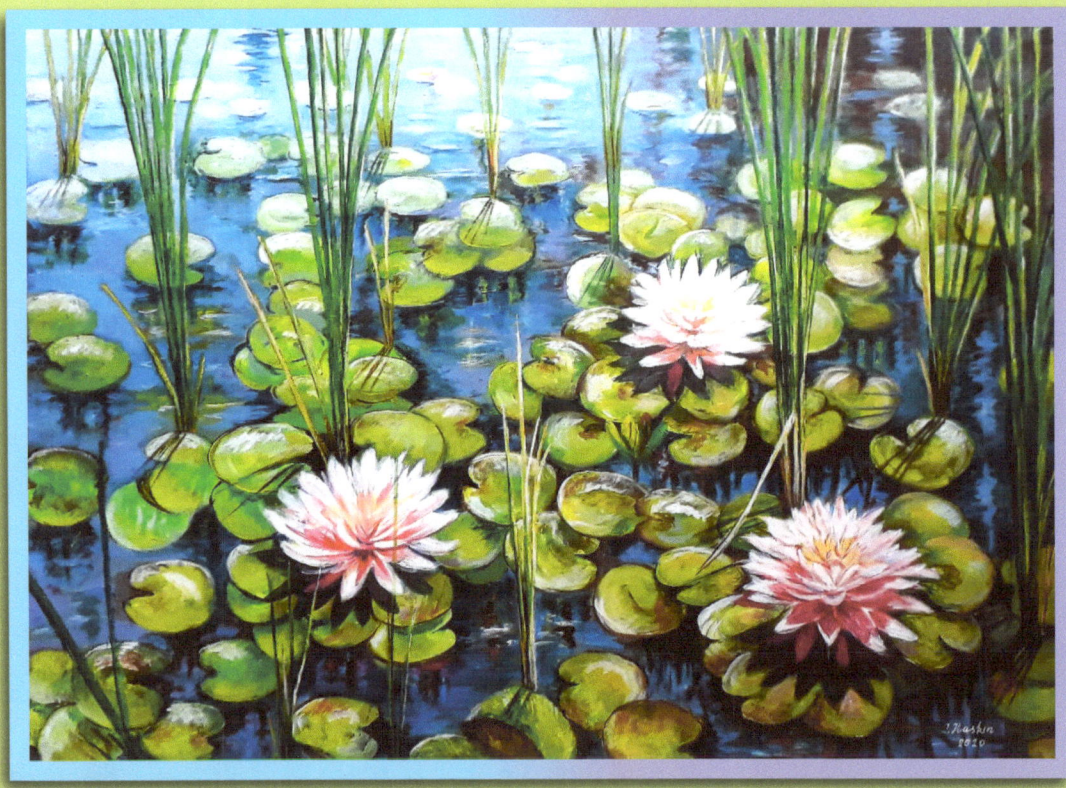

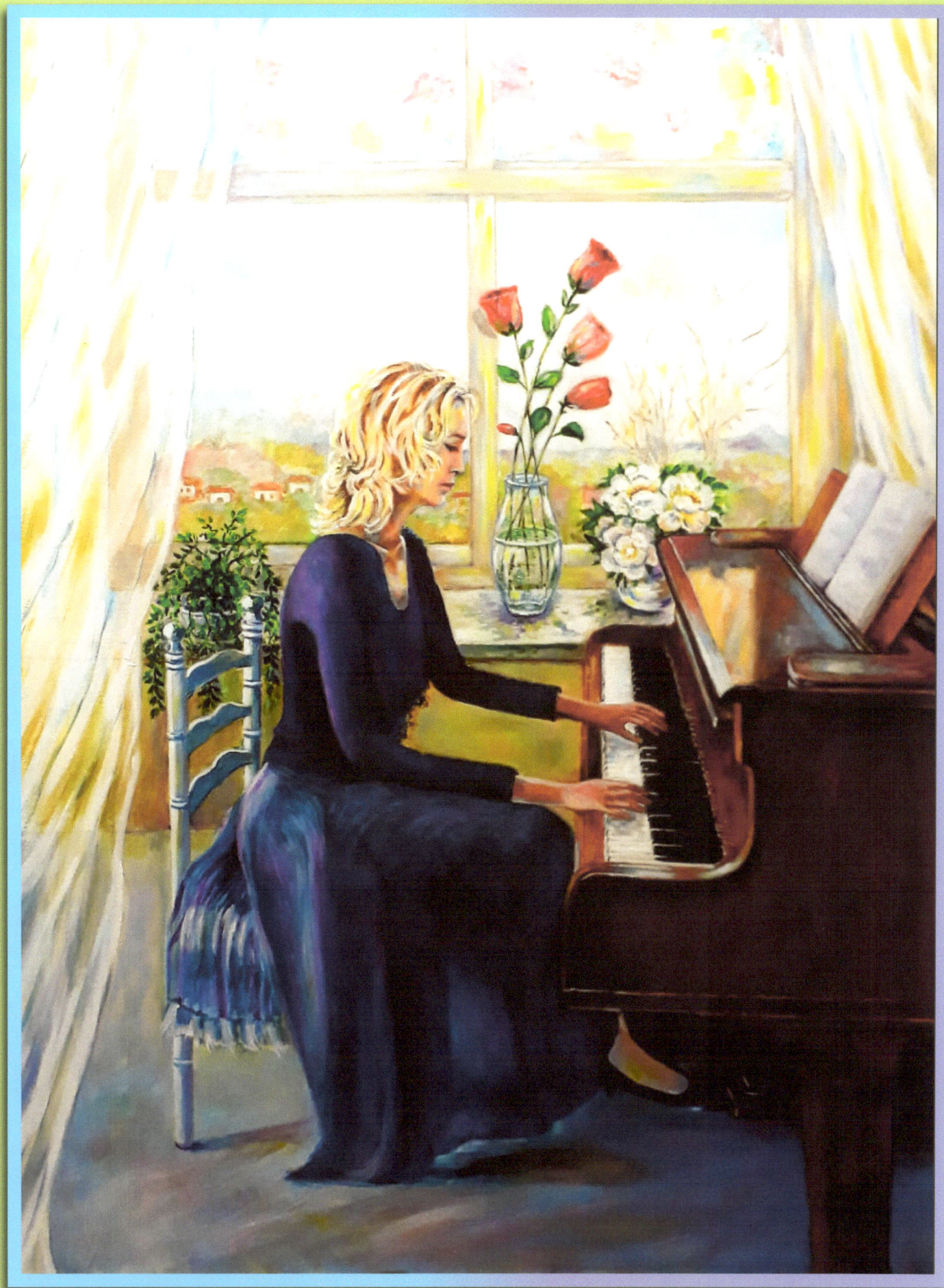

Ricki Maissy

- Painting
- 33artricky@gmail.com
- www.artdoxa.com/users/maissymaissymaissy/profile
- instagram: Rickimaissy

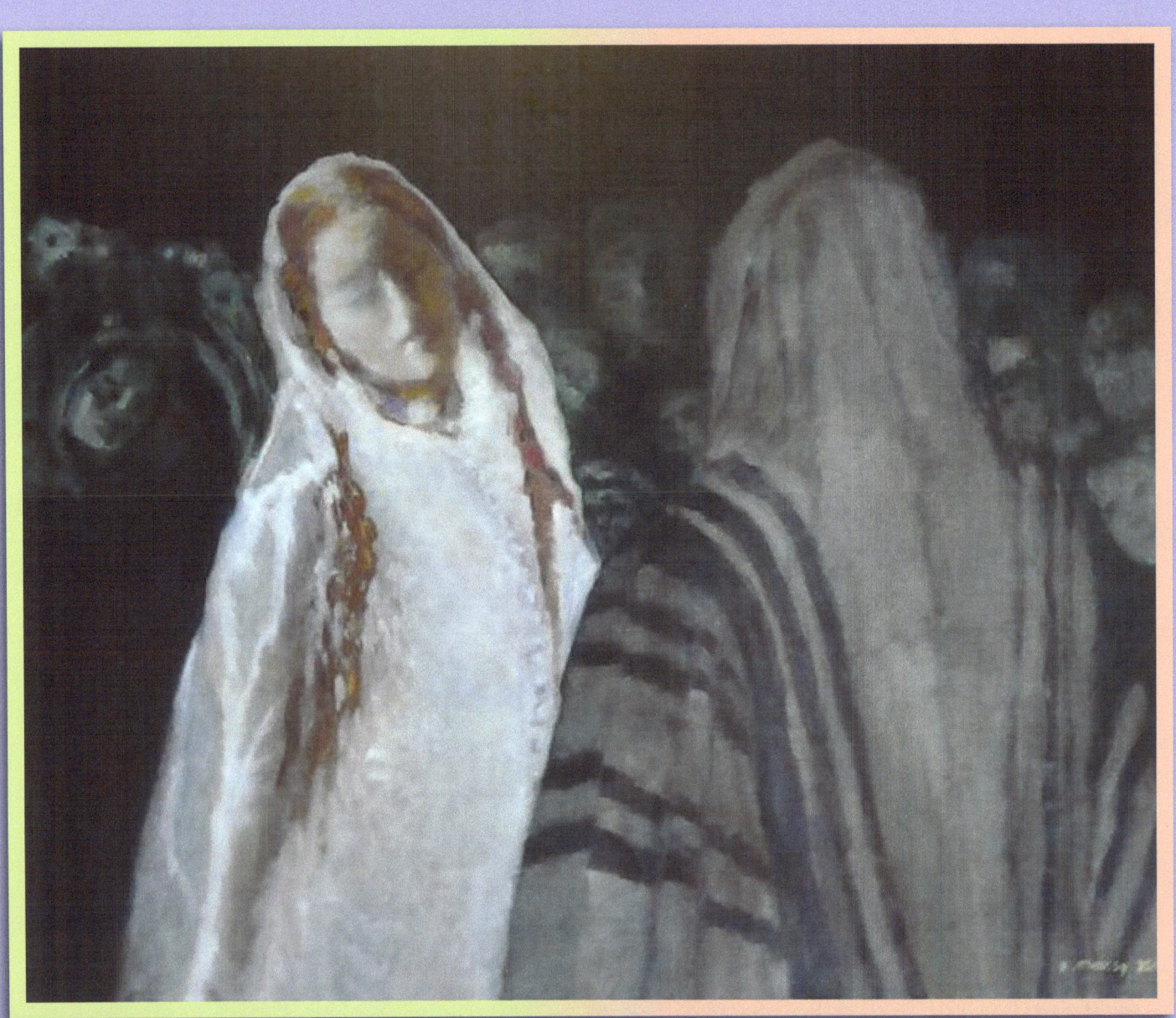

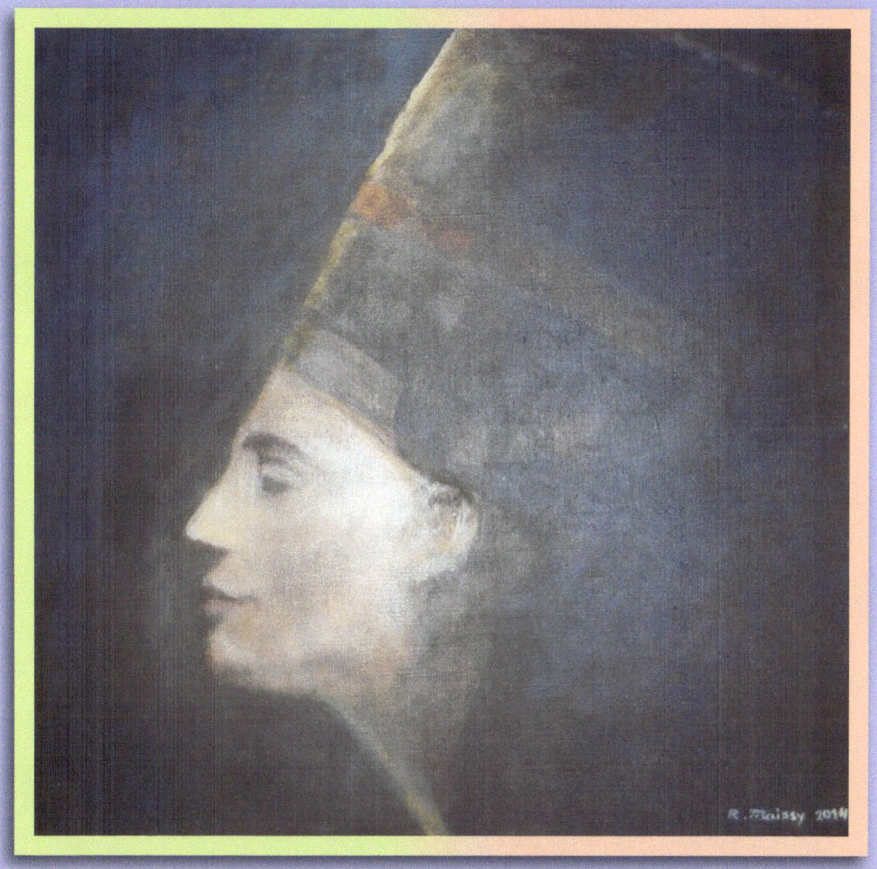

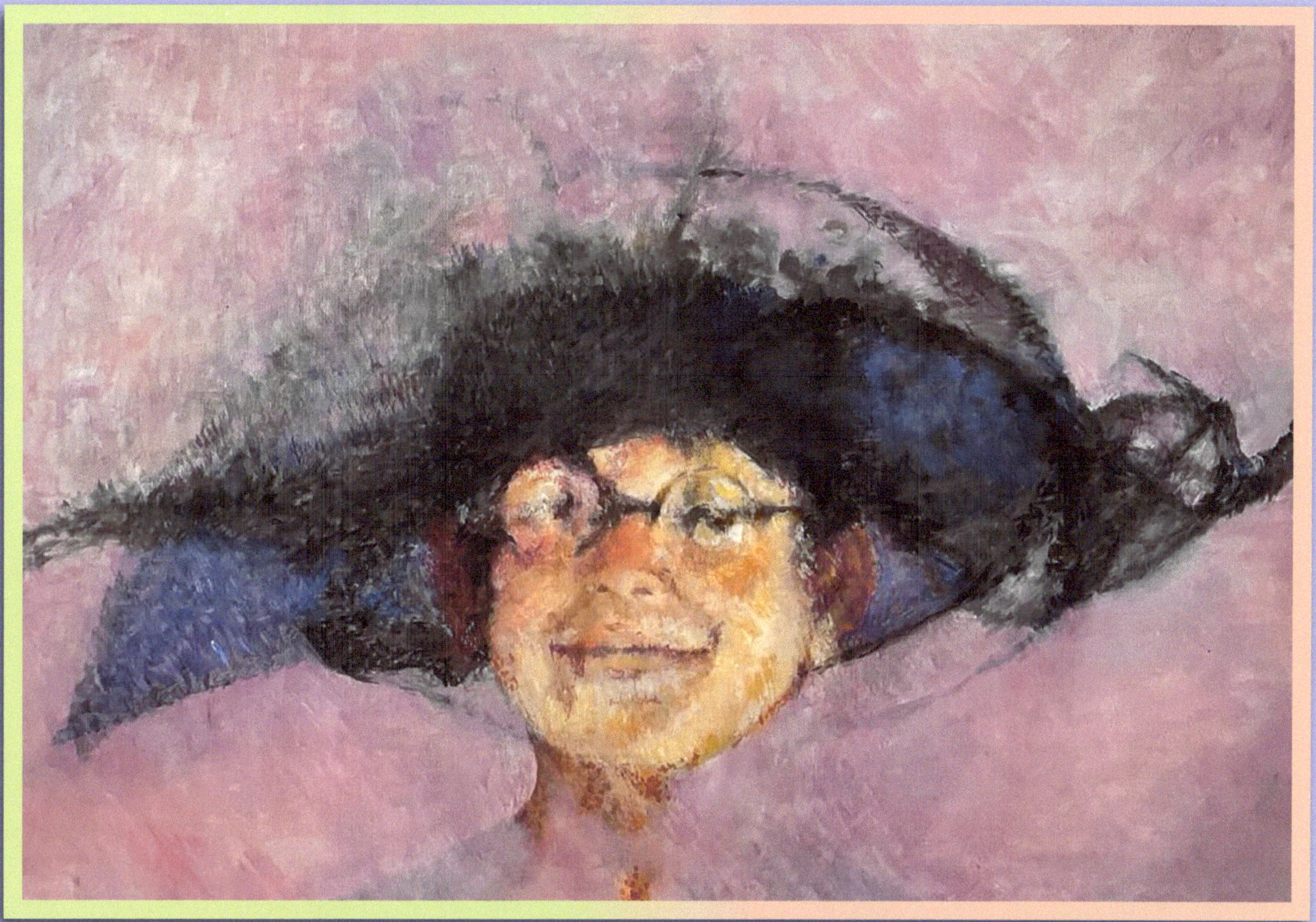

Tammara Or

- Painting
- tamamra.or.slilat@gmail.com

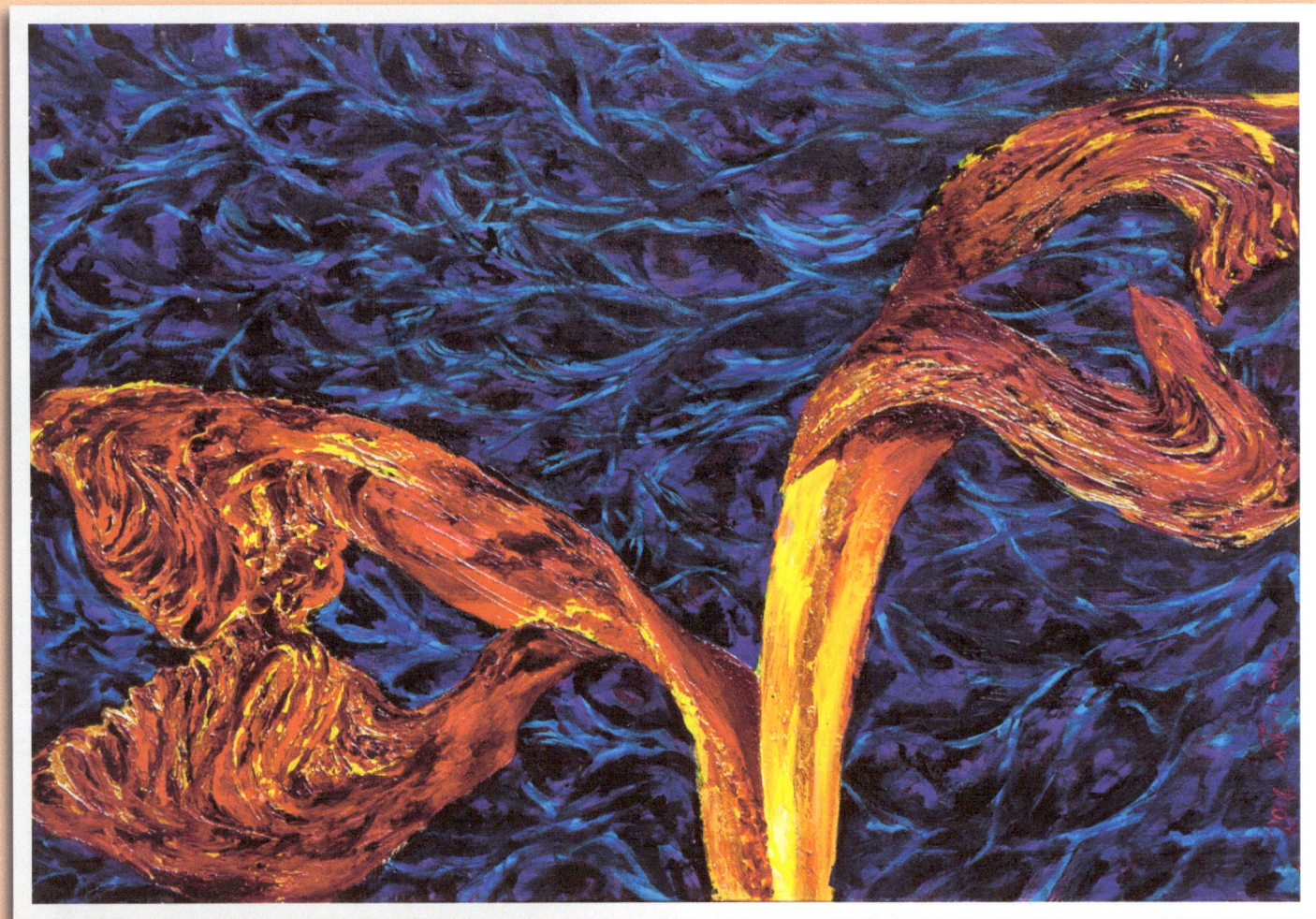

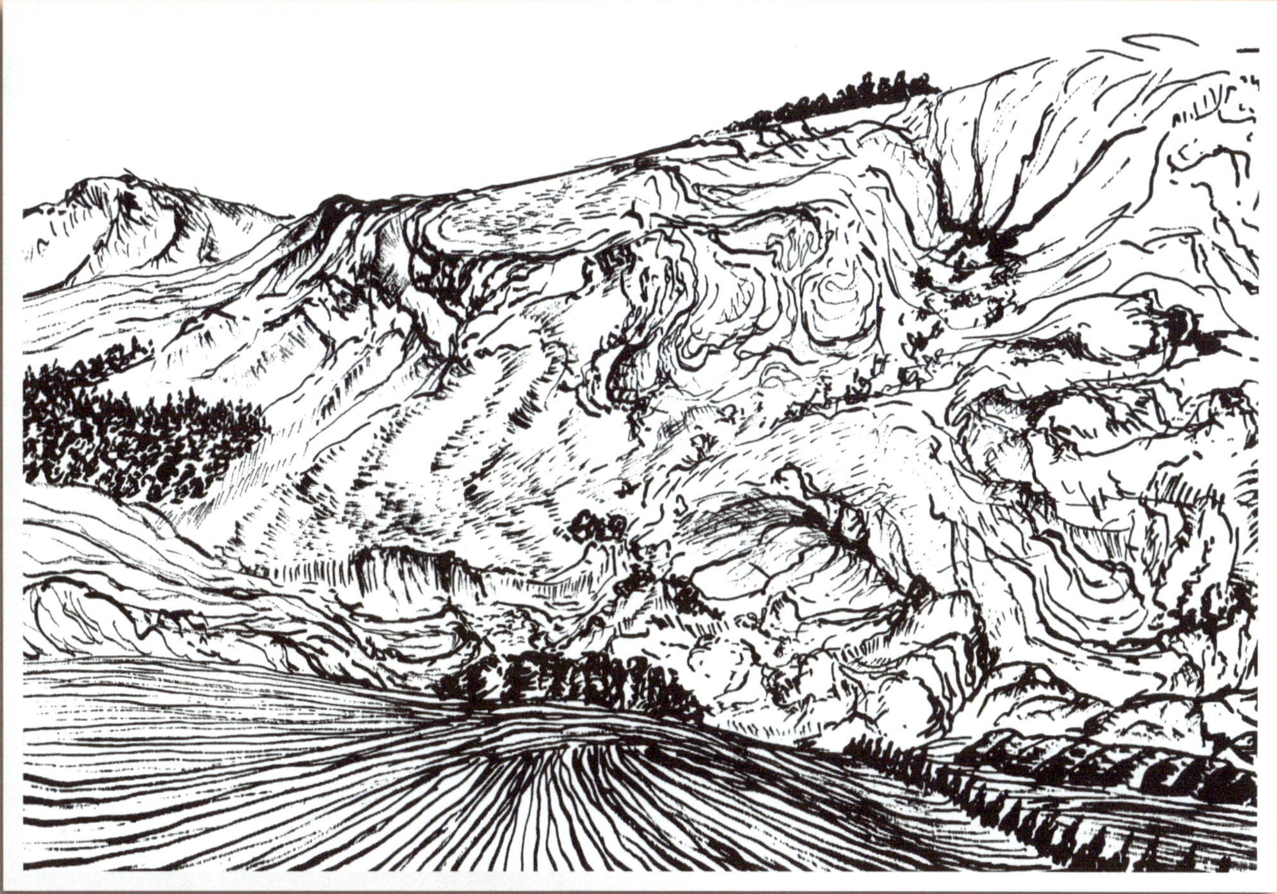

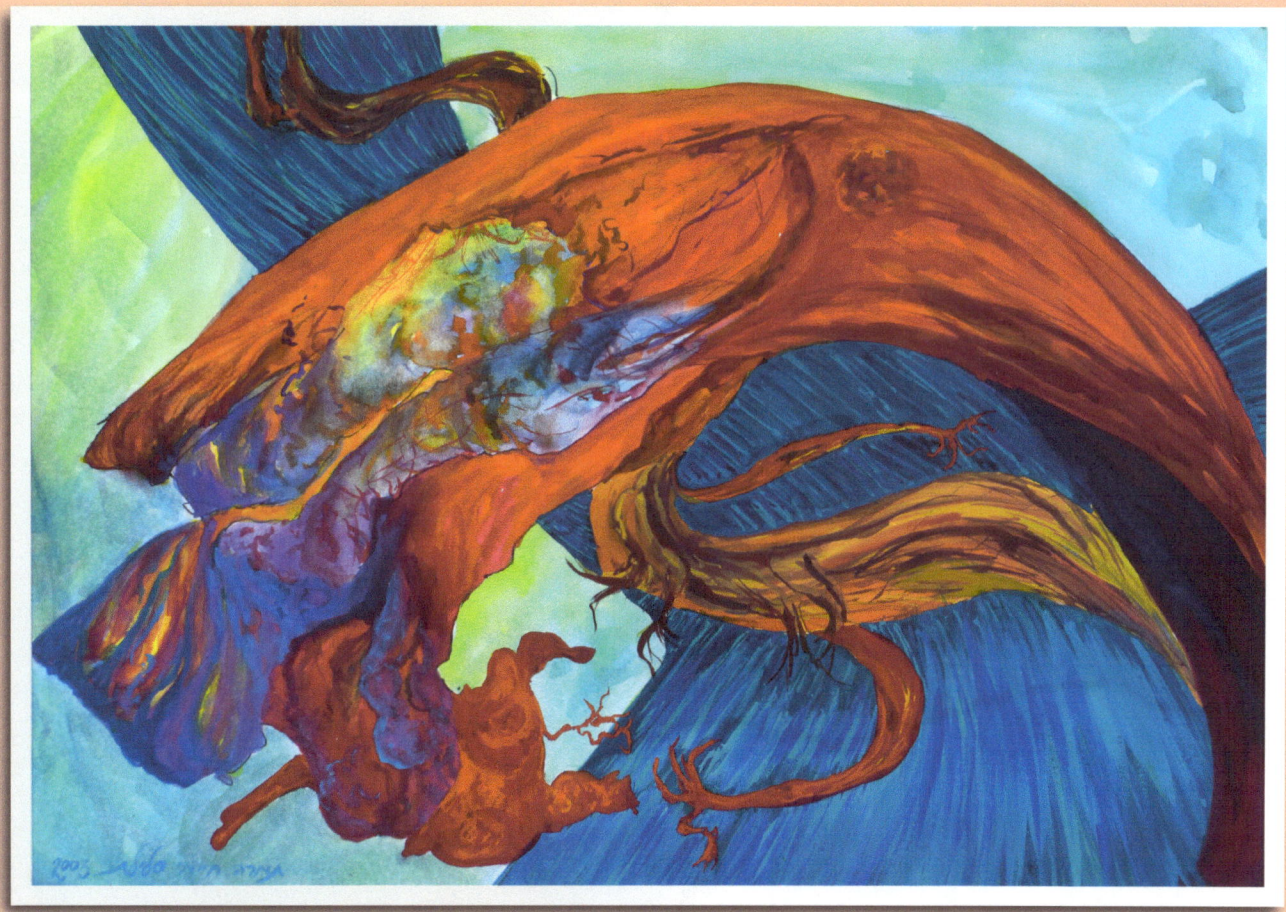

Ishay Rossano

- Painting
- rossano.ishay@gmail.com

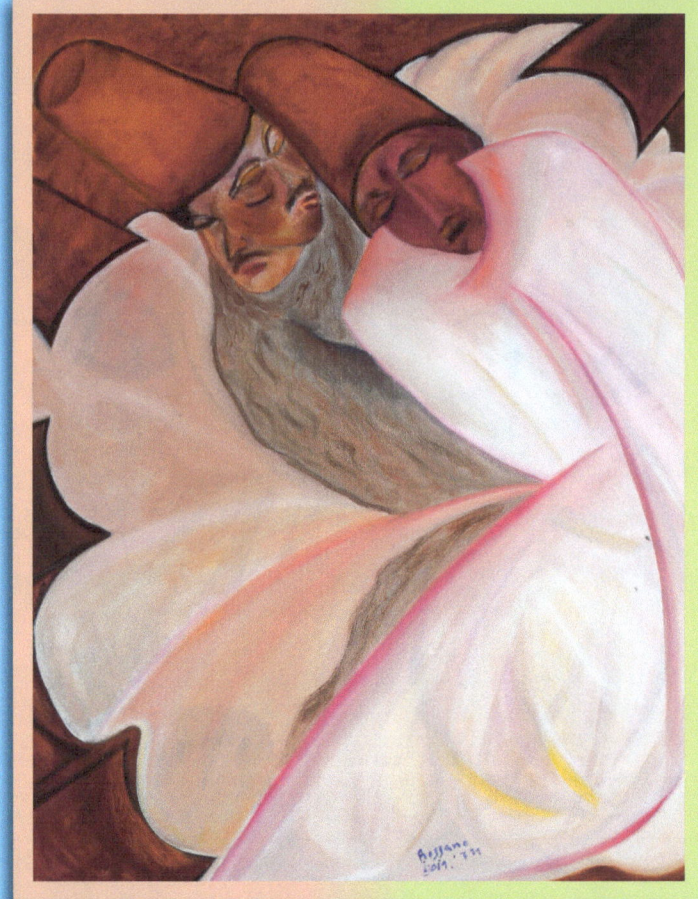
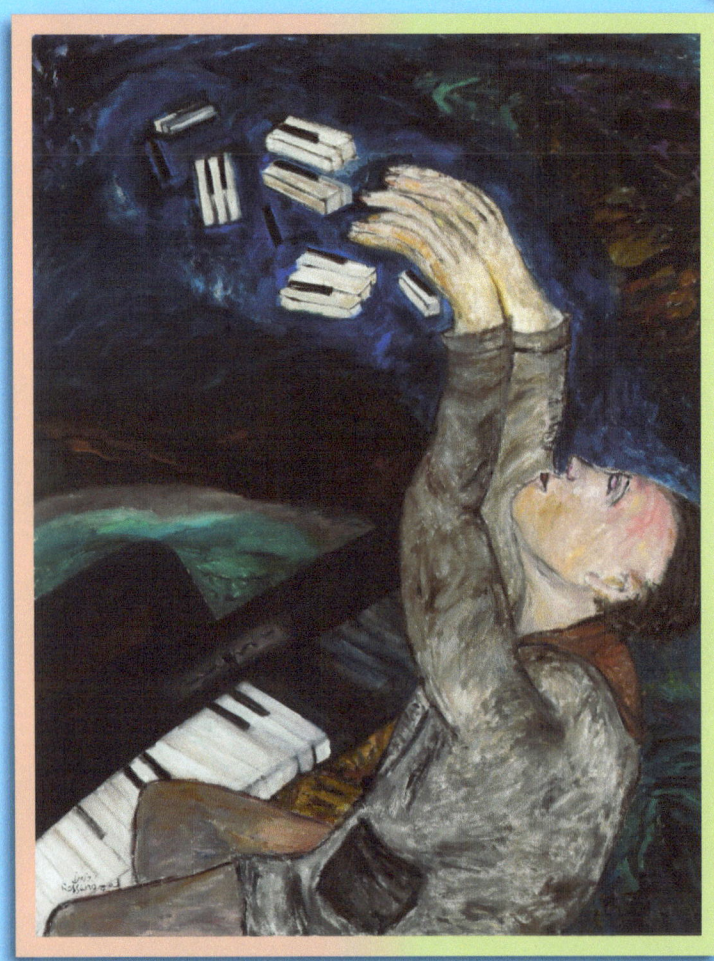

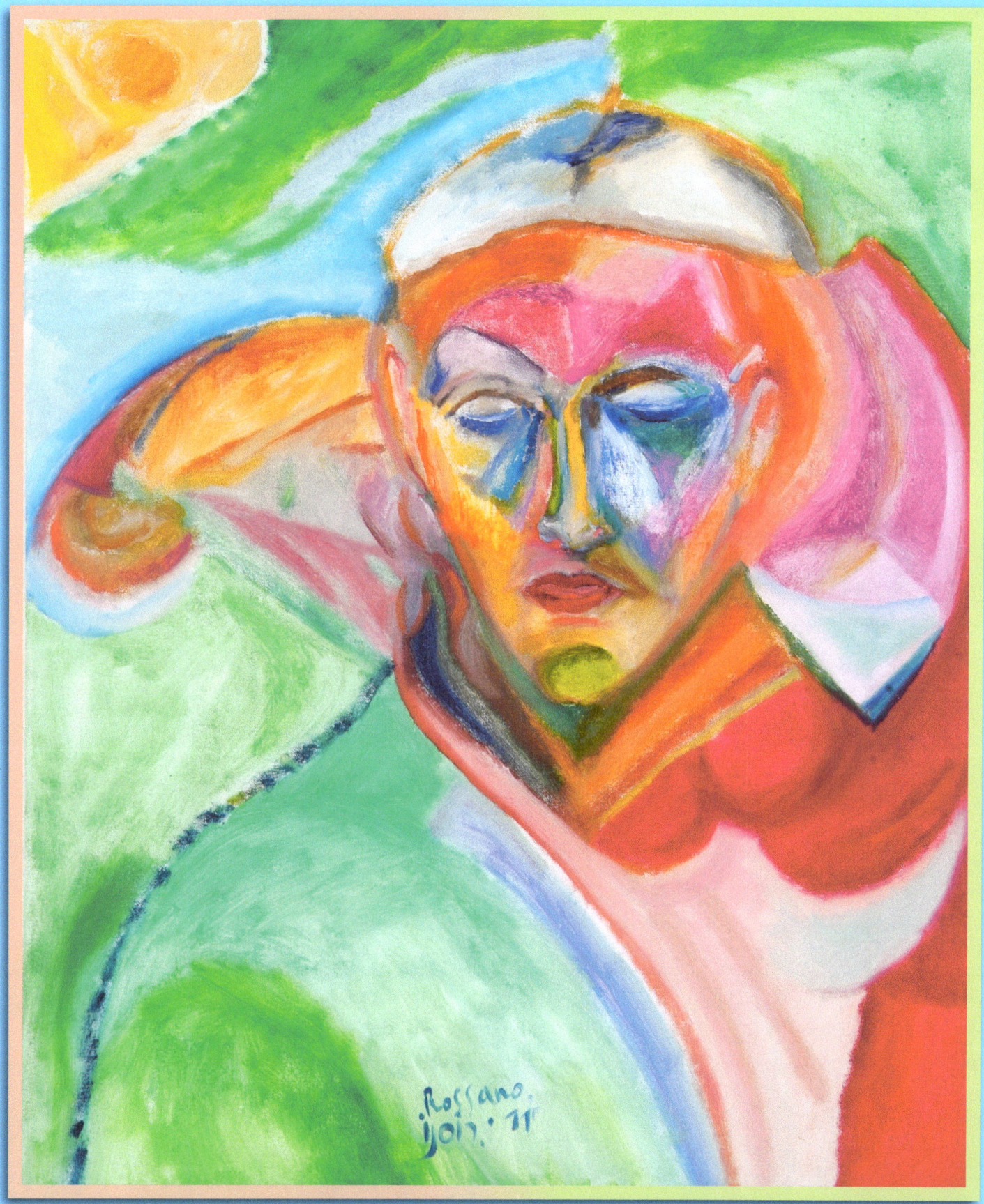

Liora Shaham

- Painting
- liorashaham@gmail.com

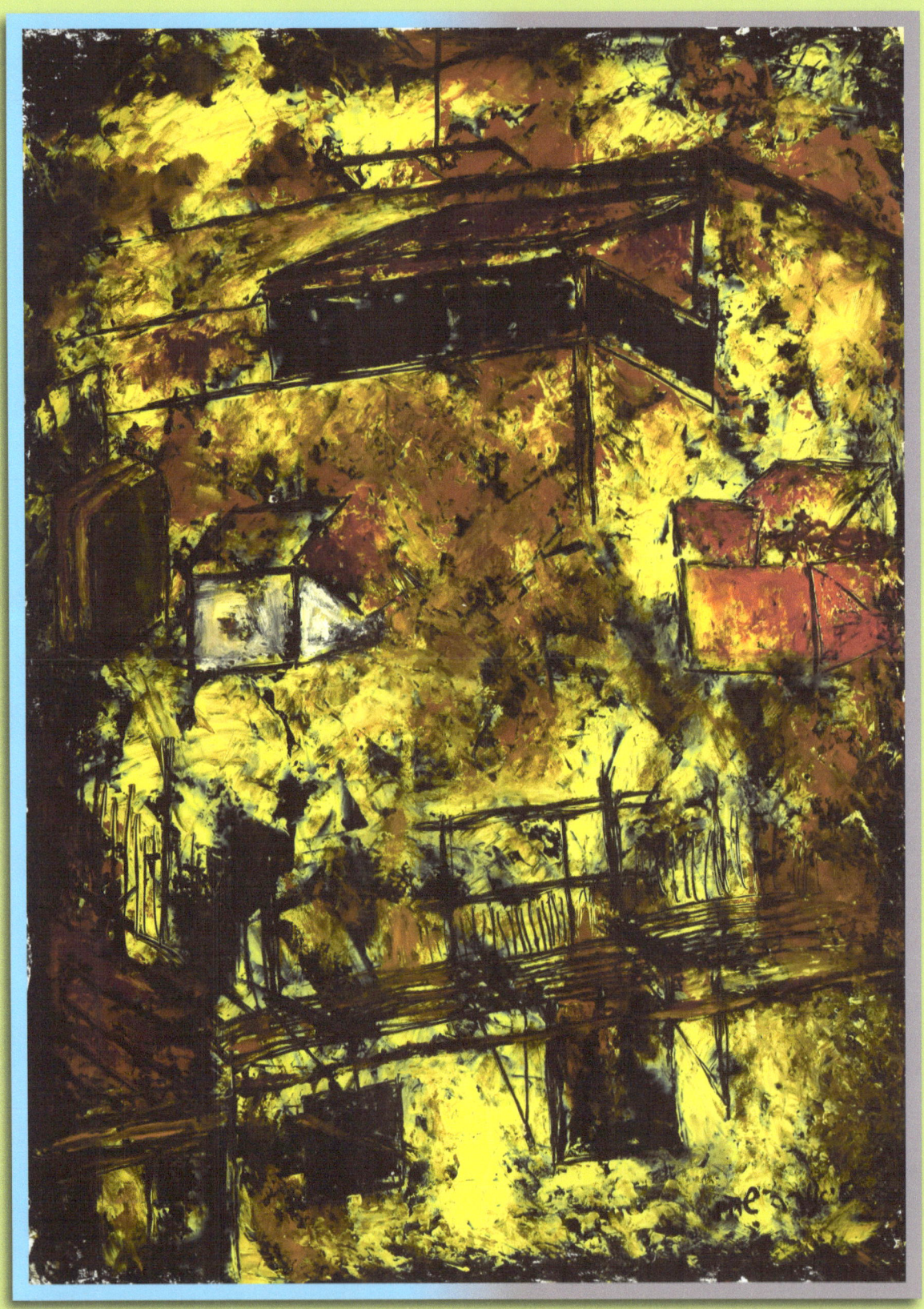

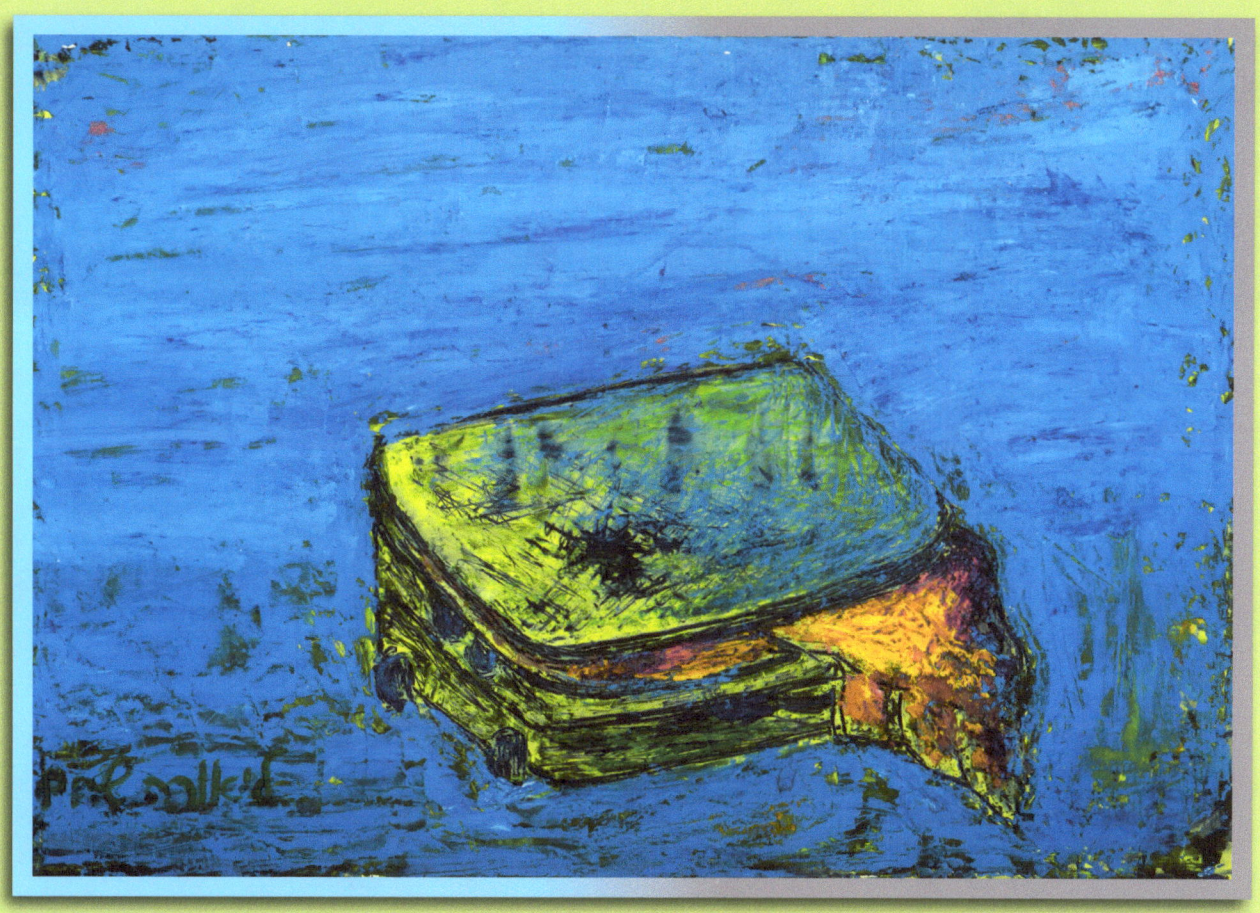

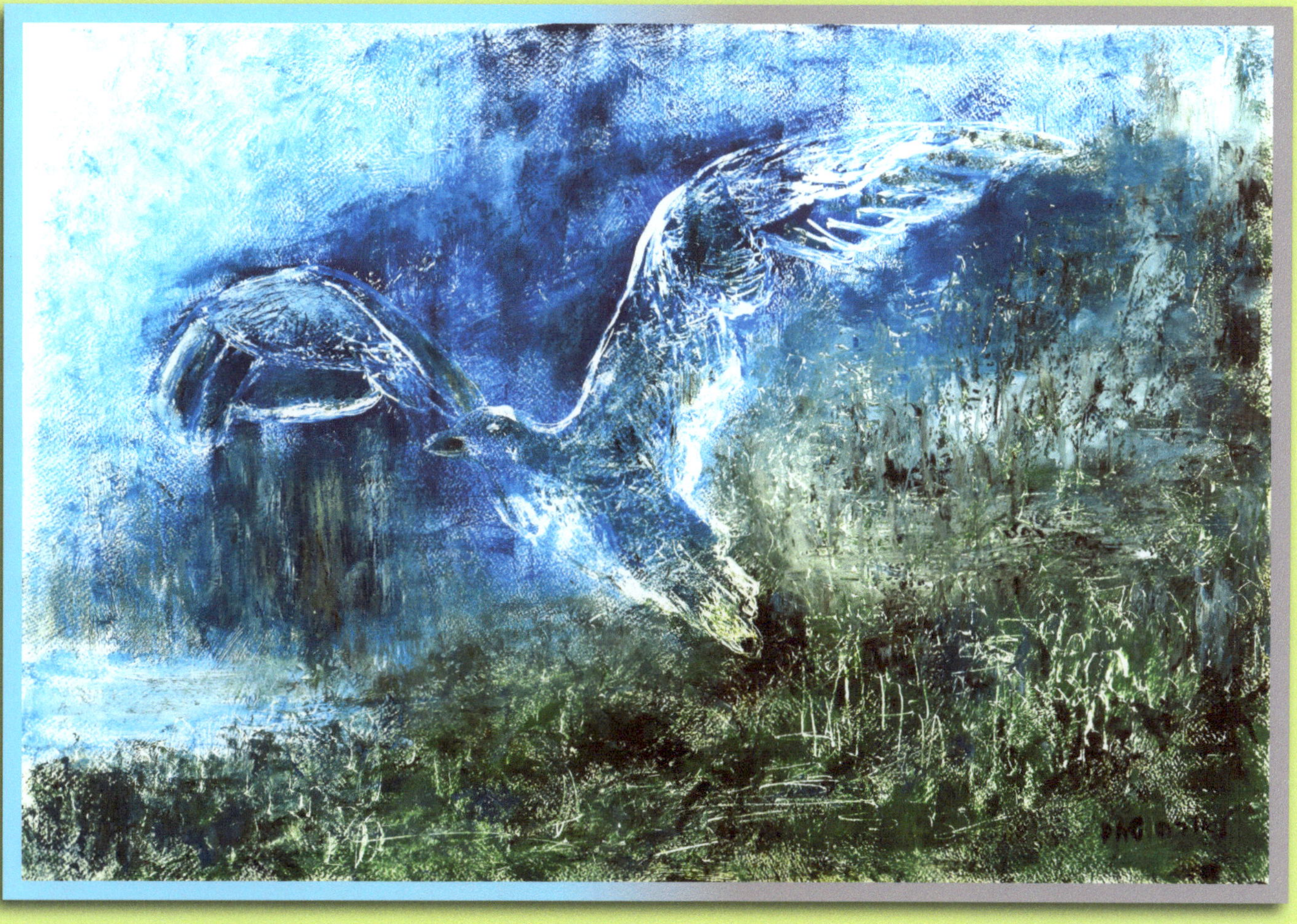

David Tsinman

- Drawing and painting
- dtsinman@yahoo.com

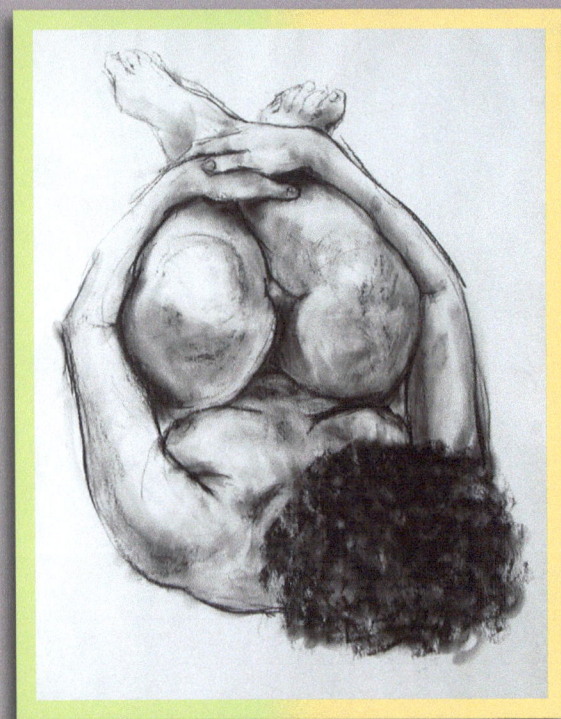
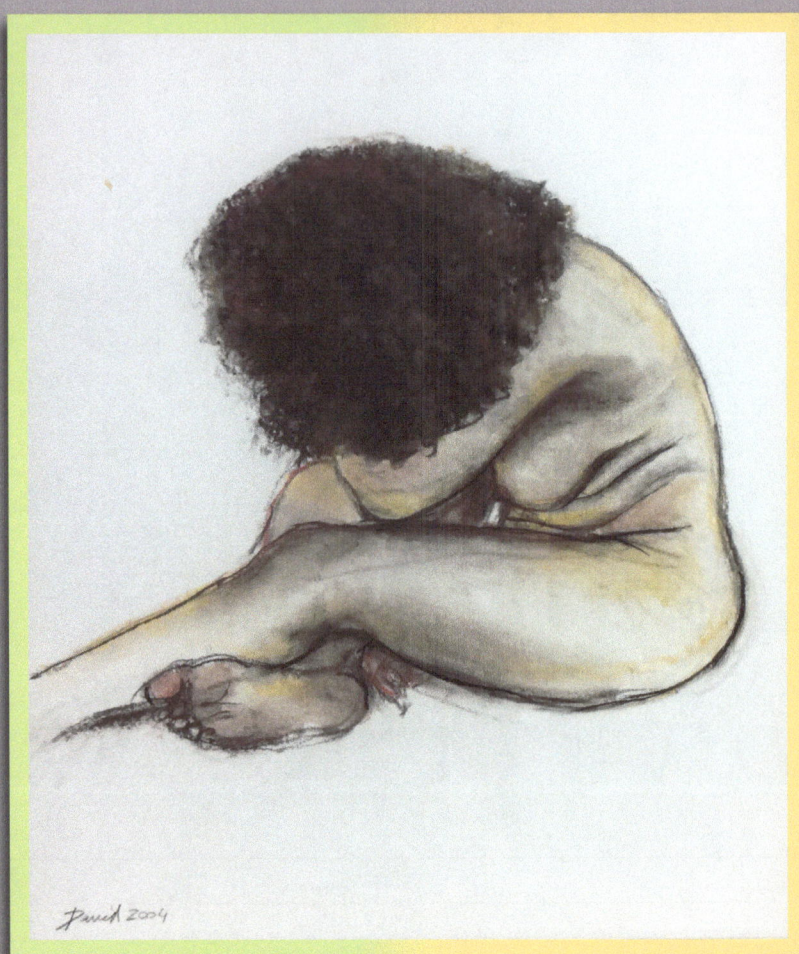
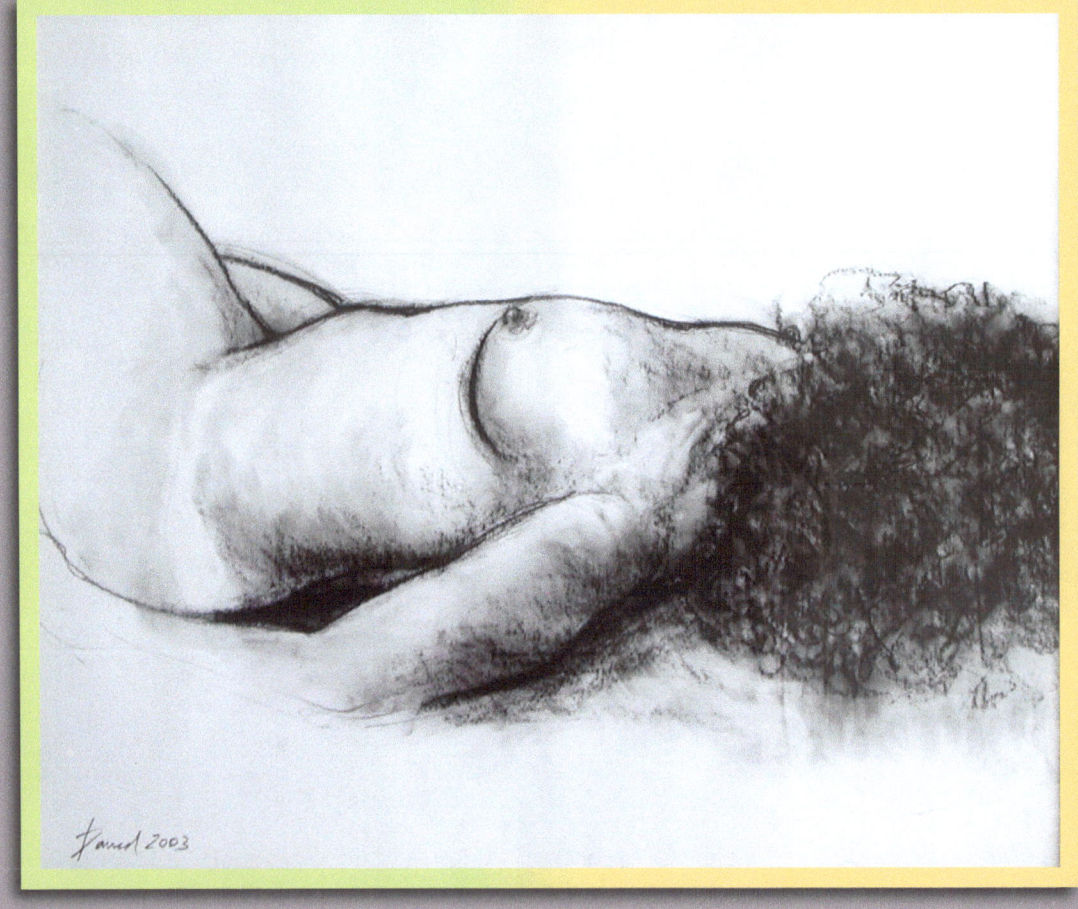

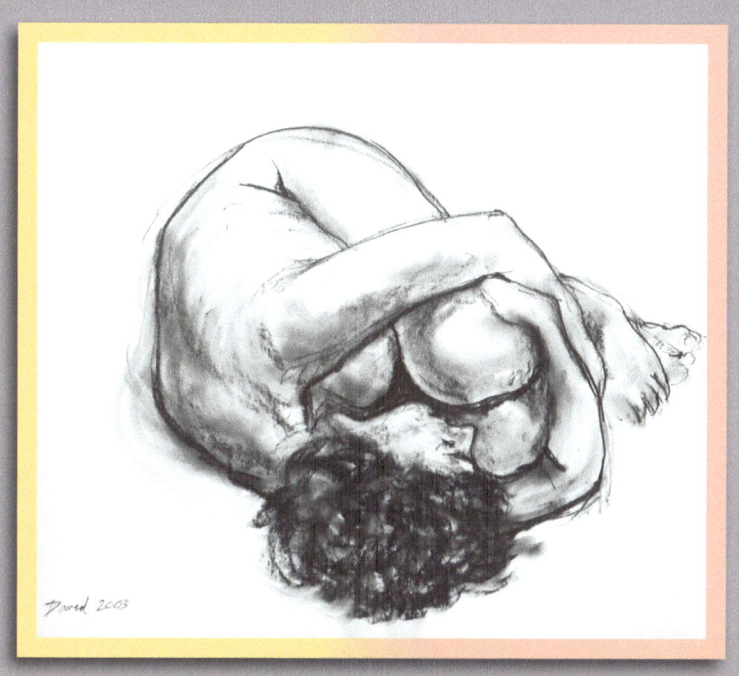
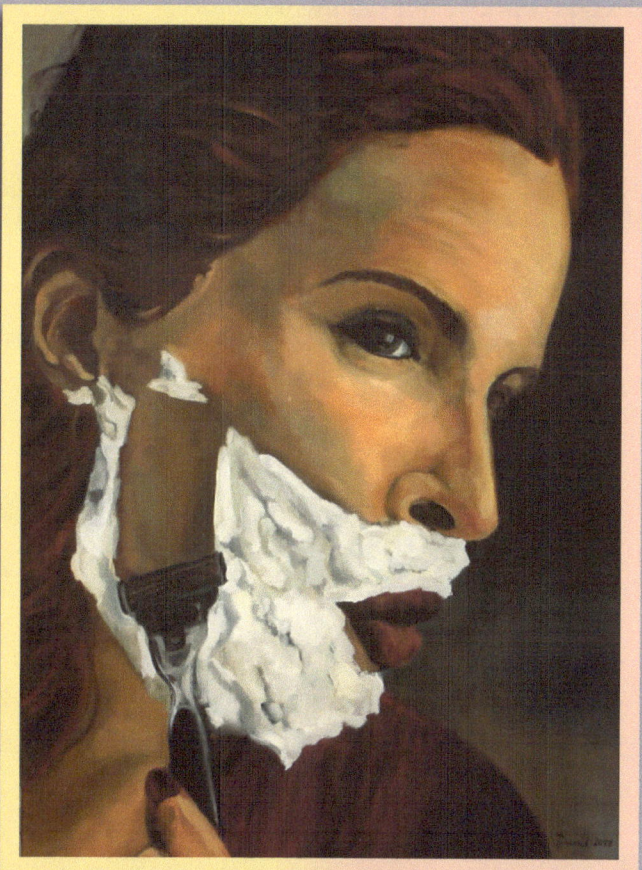
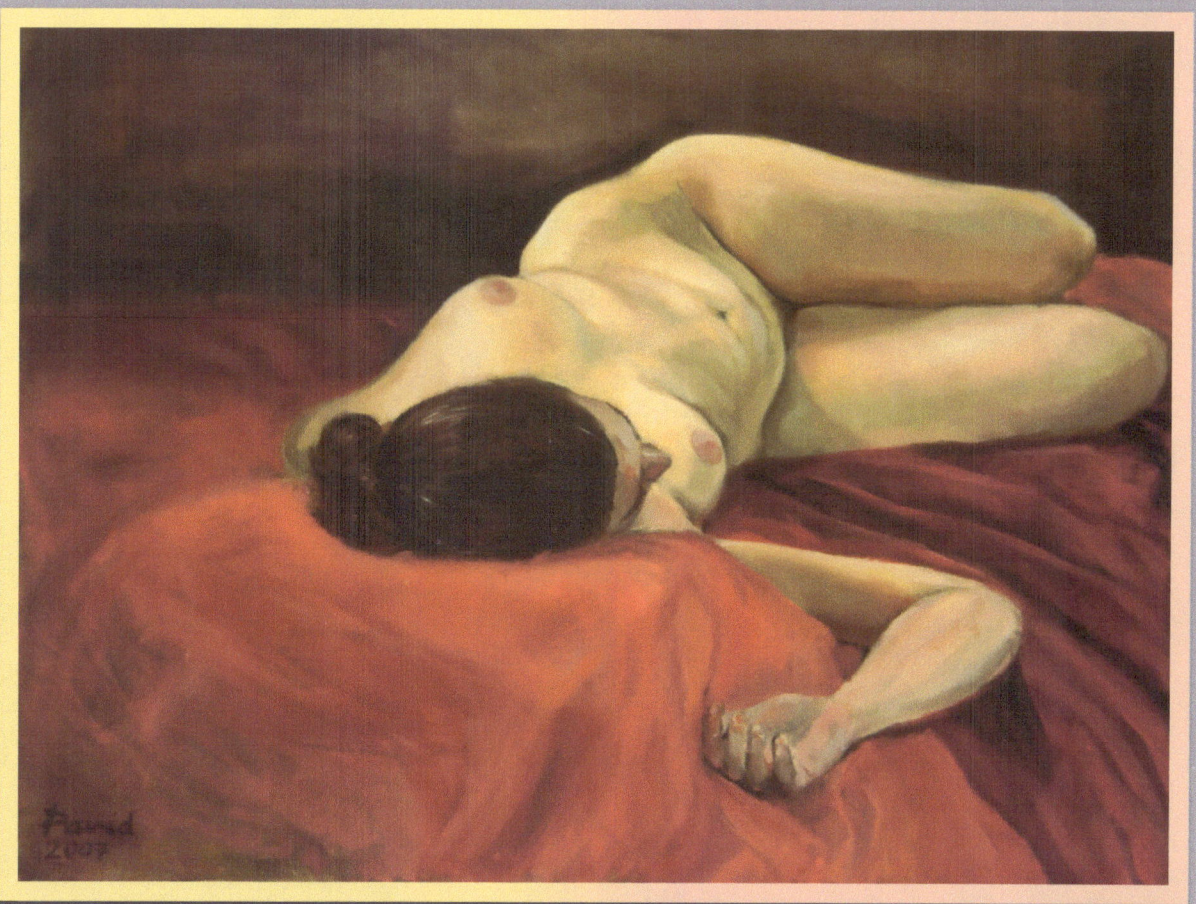

Anna Tufeld

- Art Photography
- anna.tufeld1@gmail.com

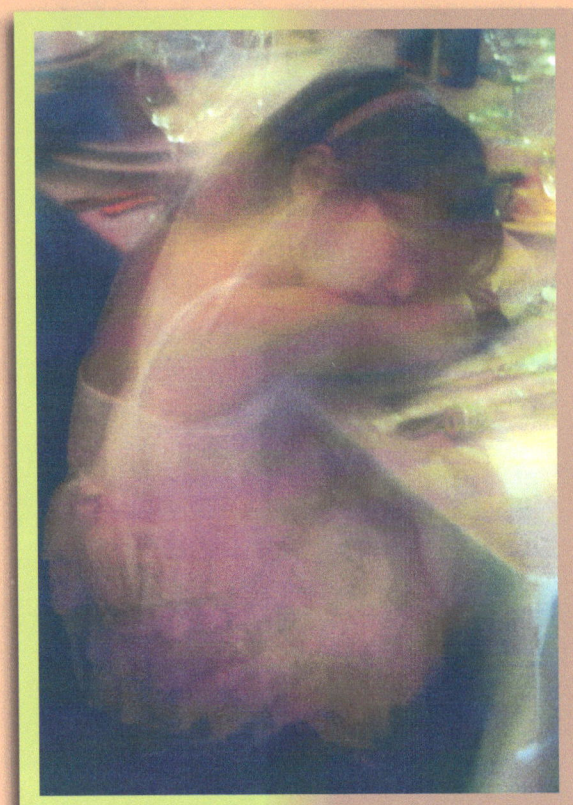
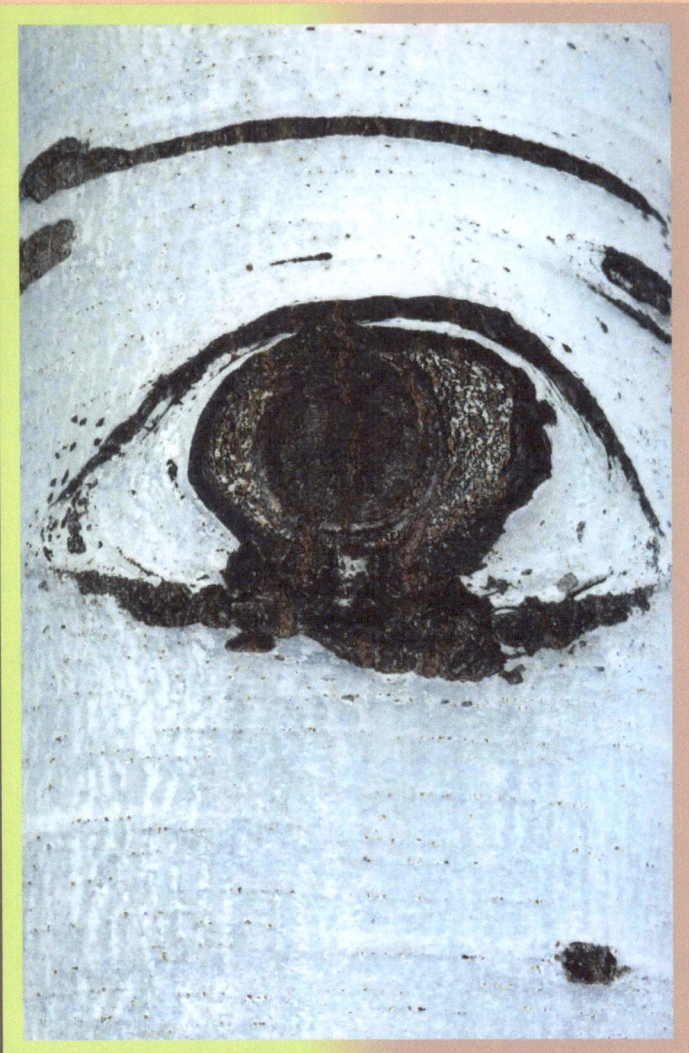
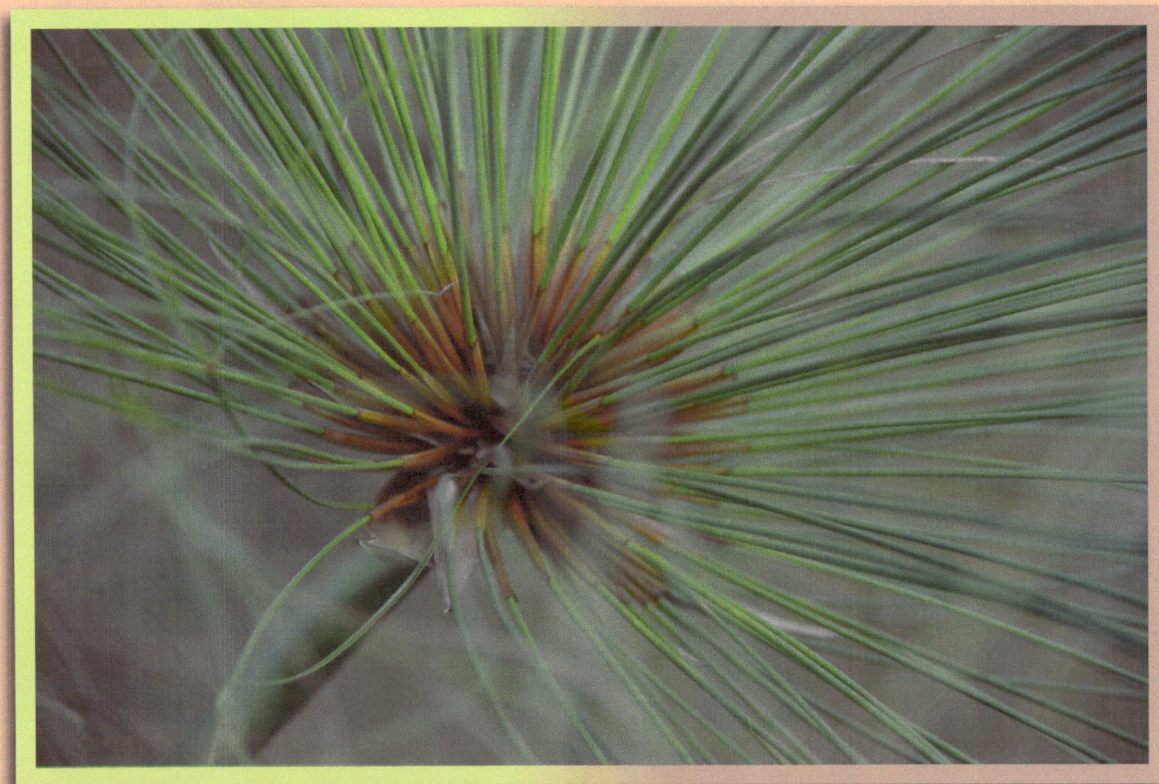

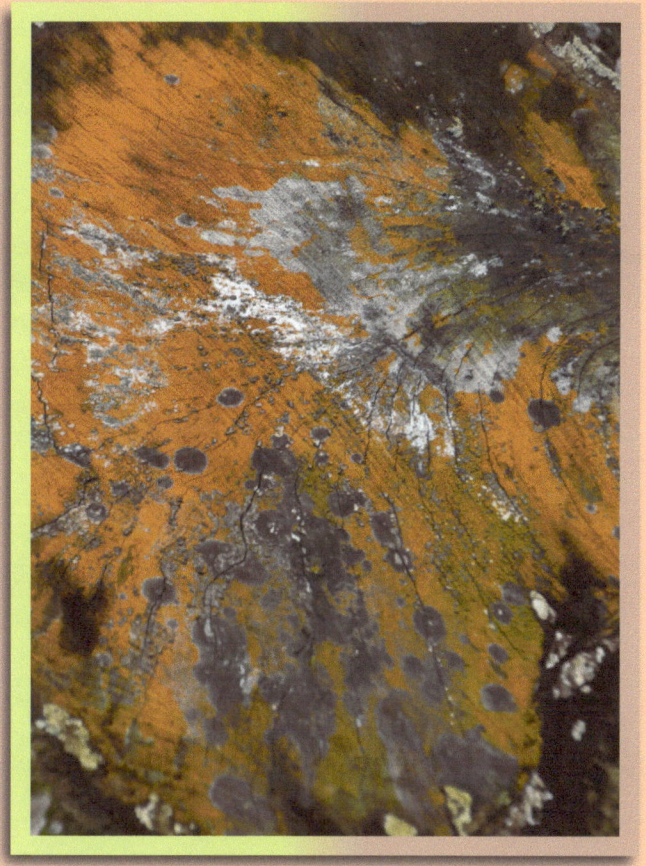
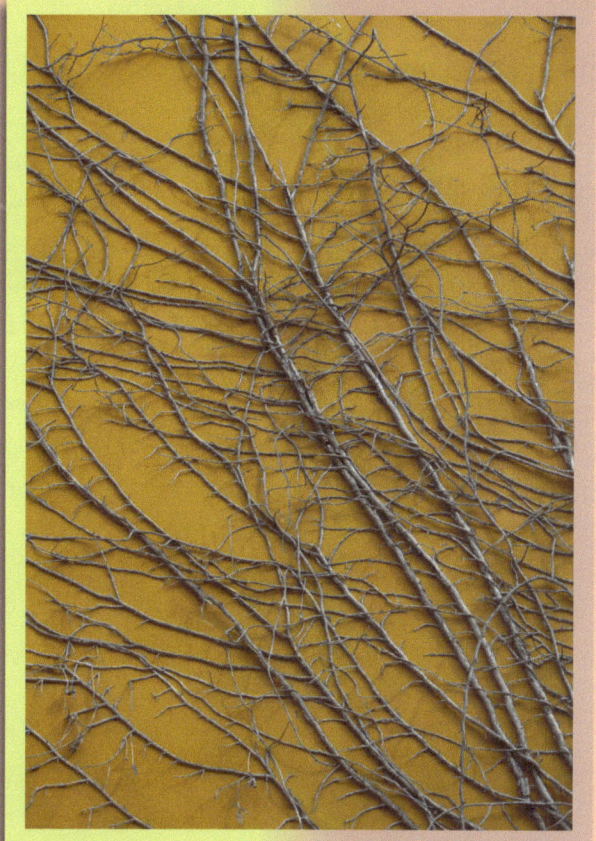

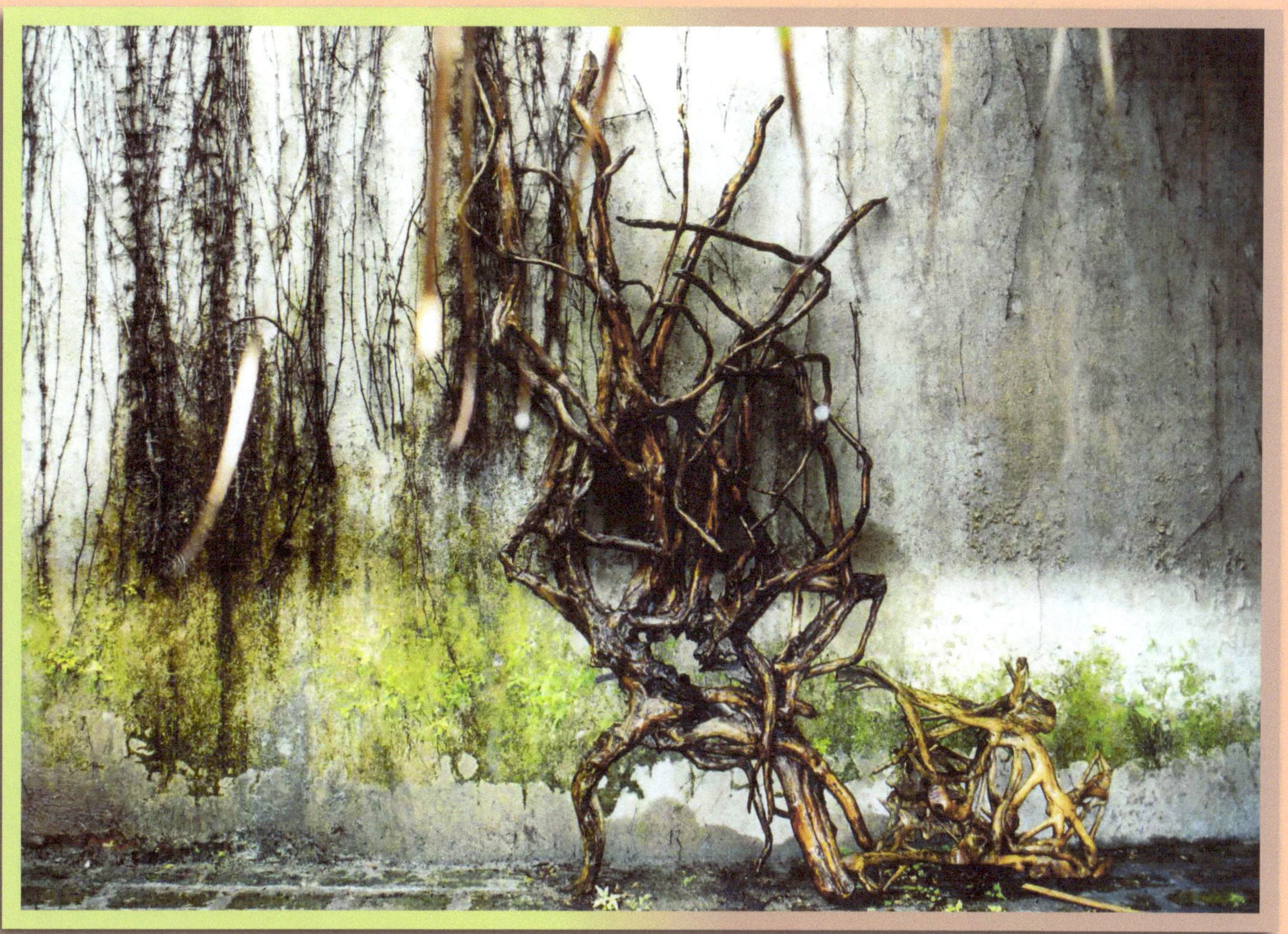

Netiva Caftori

- Painting
- netivac@gmail.com
- arv.neiu.edu/~ncaftori/
- www.netiva.free.fr

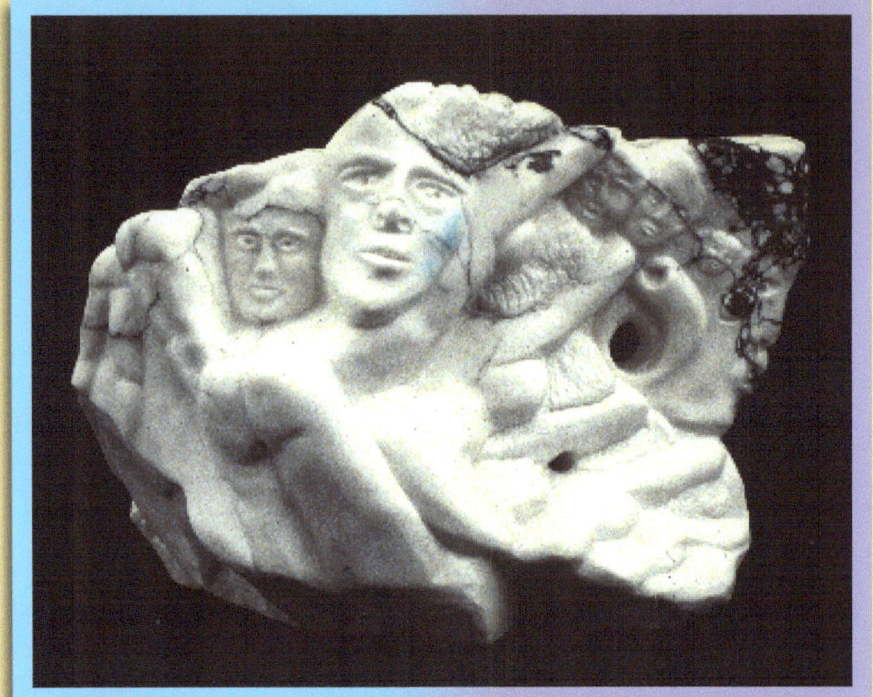

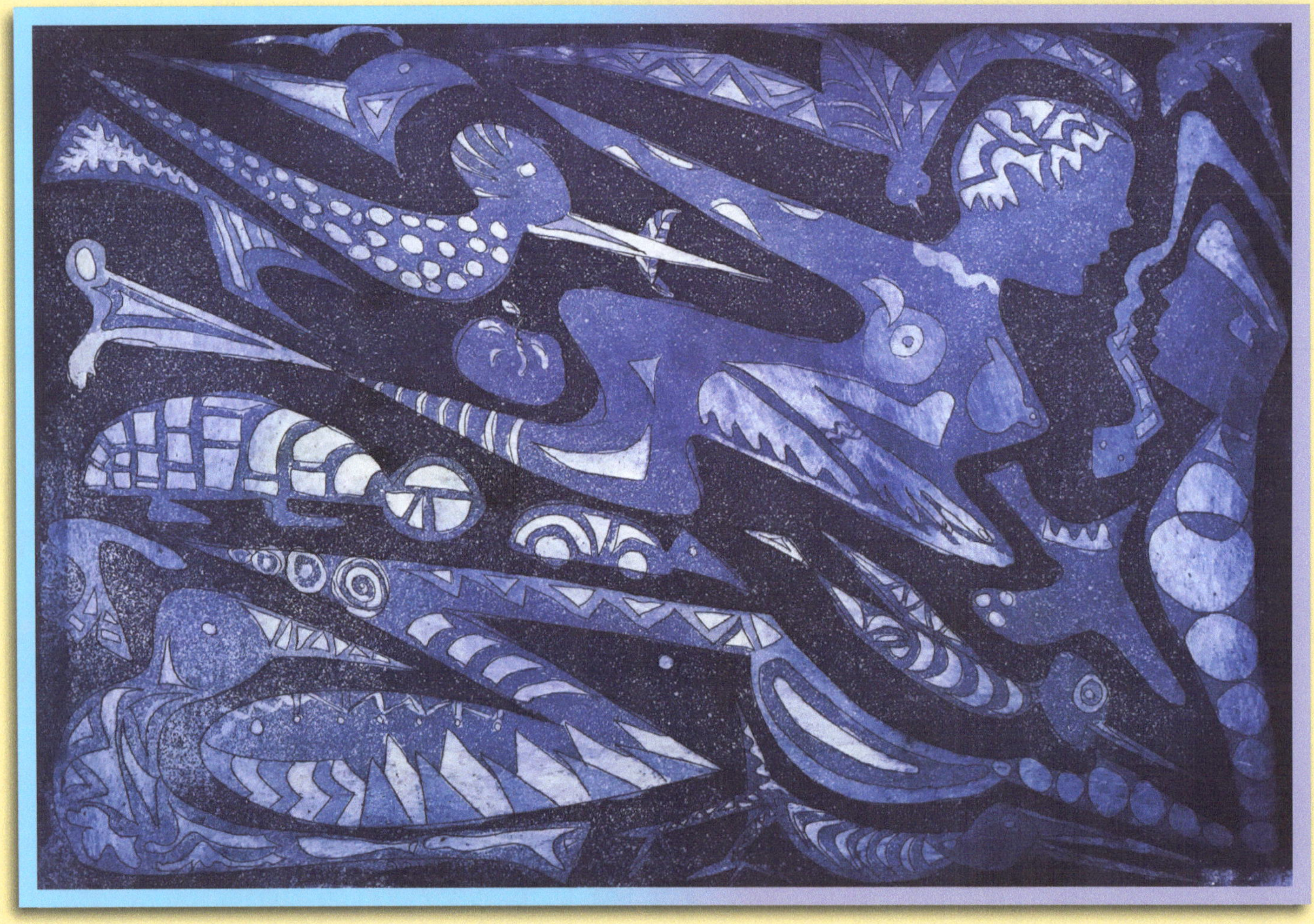

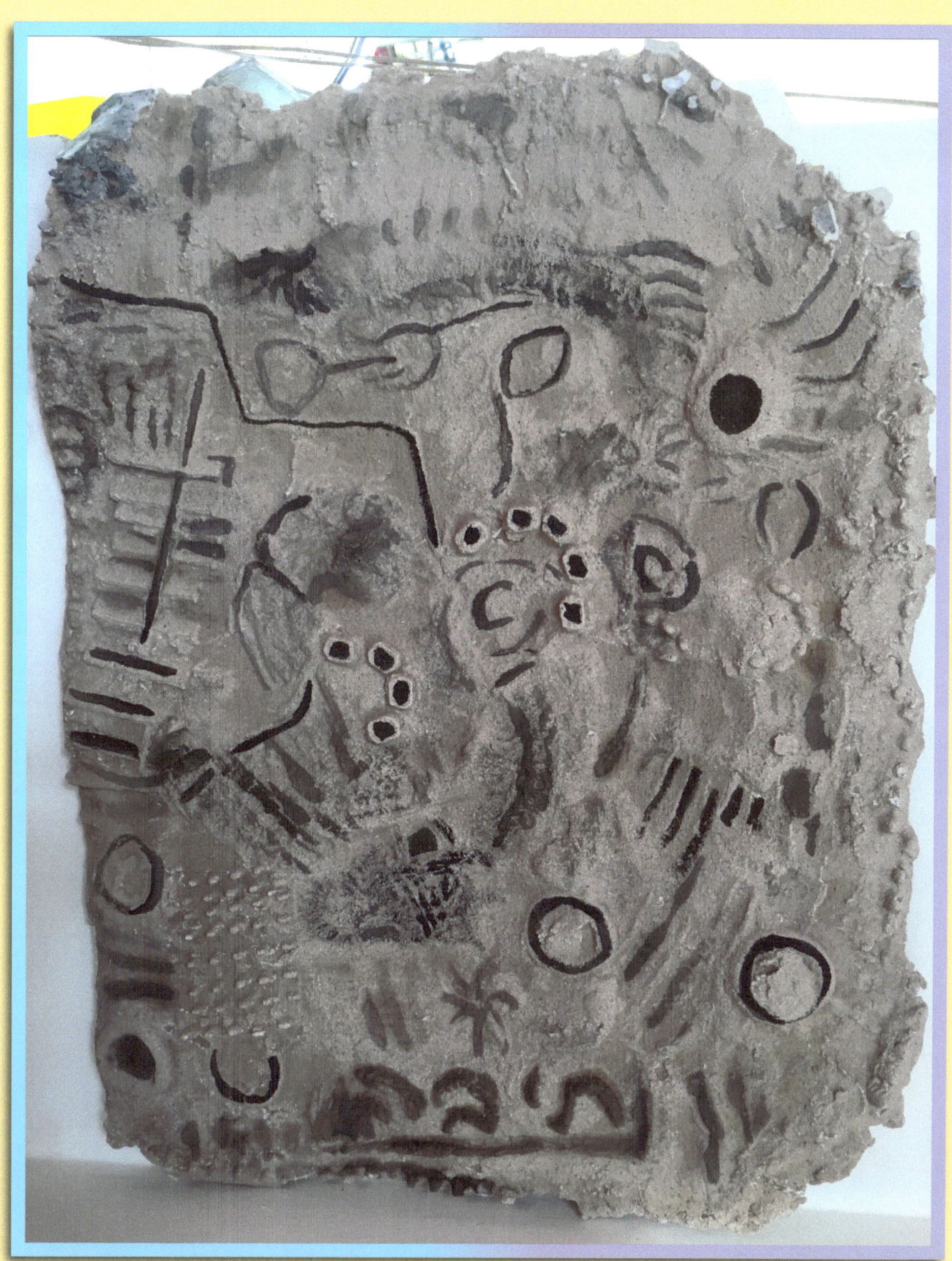

Varda Breger

- Painting and poetry
- varda@vbreger.com
- www.vbreger.com
- instagram: vardabreger
- facebook: Varda Breger

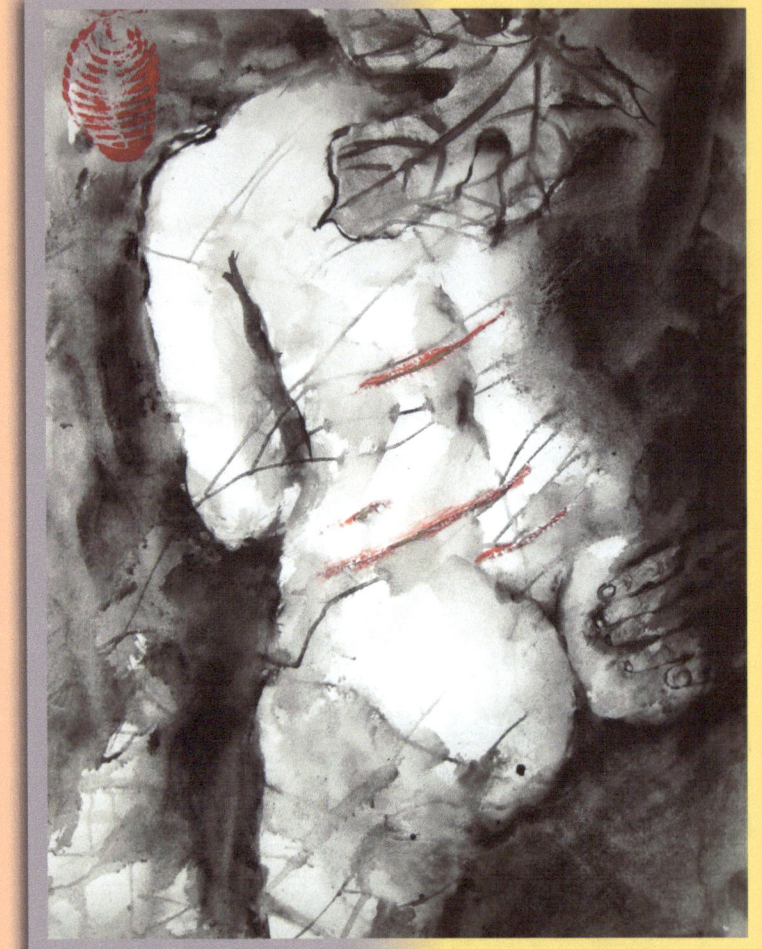

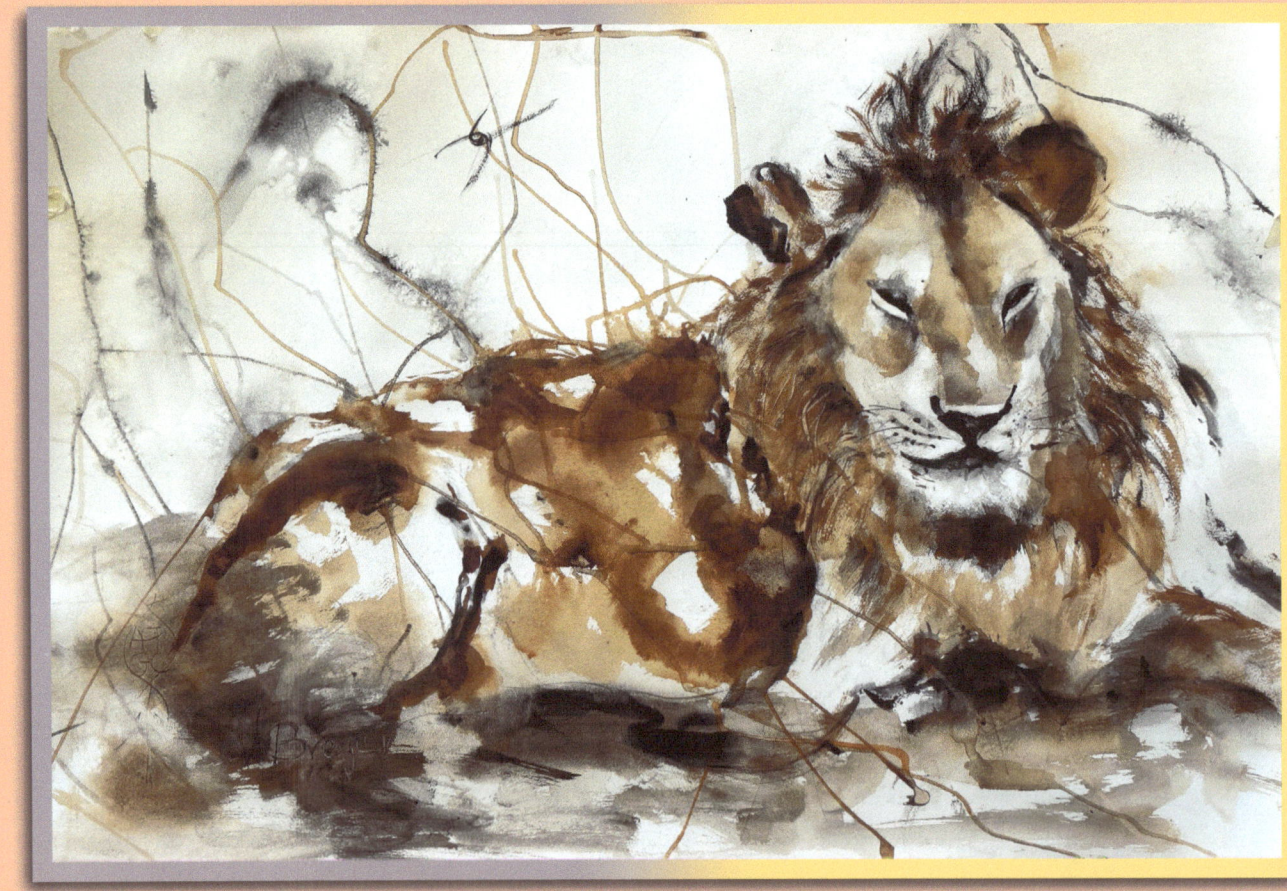

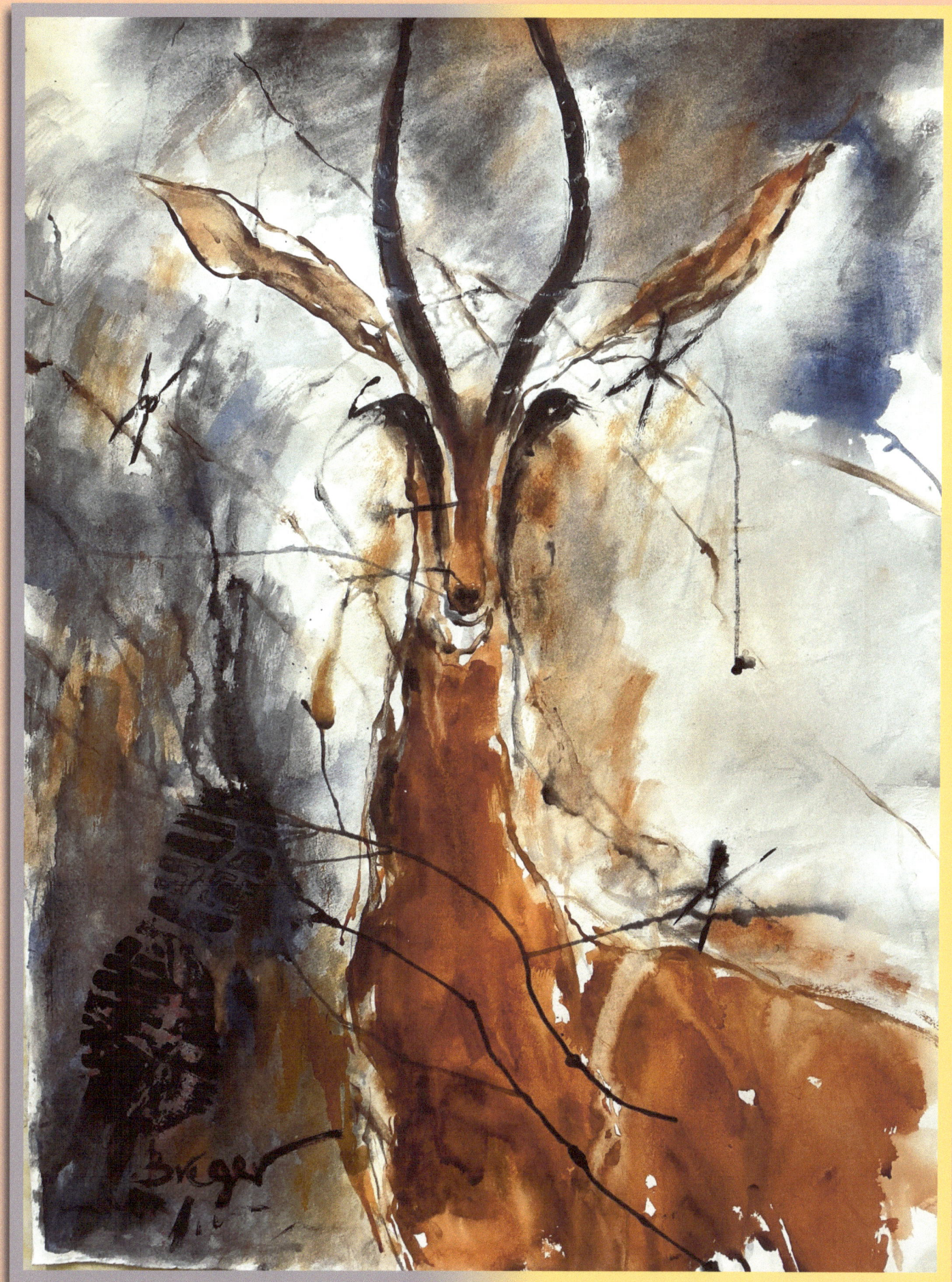

www.ingramcontent.com/pod-product-compliance
Lightning Source LLC
Chambersburg PA
CBHW051223220526
45473CB00003B/1143